How to Engage with the Private Sector in Public-Private Partnerships in Emerging Markets

How to Engage with the Private Sector in Public-Private Partnerships in Emerging Markets

Edward Farquharson
Clemencia Torres de Mästle
and E.R. Yescombe
with Javier Encinas

PPIAF
PUBLIC-PRIVATE INFRASTRUCTURE ADVISORY FACILITY

THE WORLD BANK

ISBN: 978-0-8213-7863-2
eISBN: 978-0-8213-8552-4
DOI: 10.1596/978-0-8213-7863-2

Library of Congress Cataloging-in-Publication Data
Farquharson, Edward, 1962–
How to engage with the private sector in public-private partnerships in emerging markets / Edward Farquharson, Clemencia Torres de Mästle, and E.R. Yescombe ; with Javier Encinas.
   p. cm.
Includes bibliographical references.
ISBN 978-0-8213-7863-2 — ISBN 978-0-8213-8552-4 (electronic)
1. Public-private sector cooperation. 2. Infrastructure (Economics)—Finance. 3. Public works—Finance. I. Torres de Mästle, Clemencia, 1962– II. Yescombe, E. R. III. Title.
   HD3871.F37 2010
   352.2'9—dc22

                                                                        2010044905

Cover photos: © World Bank.
Cover design: Naylor Design, Inc.

CONTENTS

11. CONCLUSION   145

APPENDIXES   149

REFERENCES   167

INDEX   171

BOXES

FIGURES

TABLES

ACKNOWLEDGMENTS

This book was made possible by a grant from the Public-Private Infrastructure Advisory Facility (PPIAF). It builds on an earlier publication, *Attracting Investors to African Public-Private Partnerships*, and the authors would like to acknowledge the contributions of all those who commented on that work. The present book, *How to Engage with the Private Sector in Public-Private Partnerships in Emerging Markets*, goes beyond the earlier publication by expanding in scope and in depth on some of the key aspects to successful and sustainable public-private partnerships (PPPs), such as the various financing mechanisms for PPPs and the diversity of PPP contractual arrangements in countries with different legal traditions. This book broadens the discussion to other emerging PPP markets beyond Africa and discusses the nuances that emerge in the recommended paths when taking into account this diversity. It includes a wide range of case studies from several regions and sectors and illustrates the different activities involved in transforming a desirable project in a government's eyes to an attractive investment opportunity for a private partner, and ultimately into a PPP project that would benefit all parties involved.

Many people have contributed valuable comments and feedback to make this book as complete as it is, yet accessible to those interested in understanding and undertaking PPPs. The authors are particularly grateful to colleagues inside and outside the World Bank Group who dedicated many hours to provide detailed and constructive comments on the individual chapters and whose contributions have resulted in a stronger and richer book. They include Jeff Delmon, Vicky Delmon, Katharina Gassner, Michael Gerrard, José Luis Guasch, Clive Harris, Cledan Mandri-Parrot,

Mark Moseley, Cathy Russell, and Derek Woodhouse. Special thanks to Michael Gerrard and Mark Moseley also for the many hours spent discussing and brainstorming on many fine points of the whole subject. Many thanks as well to Karina Izaguirre and Edouard Pérard for their assistance with the use of numbers and graphs from the World Bank/PPIAF Database. Any errors in the text remain the authors' sole responsibility.

The authors would also like to thank various people who helped make this book a reality. Special thanks in PPIAF to Andrew Jones for his most efficient collaboration in the finalization of the book, to Janique Racine for her guidance in the early stages of this project, and to Amsale Bumbaugh for her continuous support during the production process. Many thanks also to Janice Tuten in the World Bank's Office of the Publisher for her dedication and infinite patience throughout the production of this book.

ABOUT THE AUTHORS

Edward Farquharson works for Infrastructure UK (previously Partnerships UK), the infrastructure body recently established by Her Majesty's Treasury. Edward leads IUK's international team working with governments around the world on the establishment and implementation of public-private partnership (PPP) policies and projects. He has more than 25 years of experience in infrastructure finance in the United Kingdom, Africa, Asia, and Latin America as a private equity investor, lender, and adviser and has lived in the United Kingdom, Brazil, and Southern Africa. He trained as a project finance specialist in a leading U.K. investment bank and worked on one of the United Kingdom's first PPPs in the mid-1980s. Edward has an MBA from Manchester Business School and a degree in philosophy, politics, and economics from Oxford University.

Clemencia Torres de Mästle is the program leader for Global Knowledge and for West and Central Africa in the Public-Private Infrastructure Advisory Facility (PPIAF). Previously, at the World Bank, she was senior economist in the Energy Unit for Latin America and the Caribbean, senior private sector development (PSD) specialist in the PSD and Finance Department for the Middle East and North Africa, and a consultant in the Public Sector Management and PSD Division. Before joining the World Bank, she worked as a consultant on privatization and regulation. Her areas of expertise include infrastructure economics, institutional and regulatory issues in these markets, private sector participation, and state-owned enterprises' performance. She has written about electrification and regulation and on investment behavior in transmission. She holds a Master's degree and PhD in economics from Boston University.

E.R. Yescombe has more than 30 years of experience in various forms of structured finance, including project finance, leasing, export credits, property, and asset finance. He has been an independent consultant on public-private partnerships (PPPs) and project finance since 1998. He has advised project sponsors and government entities on the financial aspects of PPP contracts, as well as on policy issues and contract standardization. He is the author of *Principles of Project Finance* (2002), which has been translated into Chinese, Hungarian, Japanese, Polish, and Russian and is recognized as a leading work on this subject, and *Public-Private Partnerships: Principles of Policy and Finance* (2007). He was head of project finance in Europe for Bank of Tokyo-Mitsubishi and its predecessor, Bank of Tokyo. (See www.yescombe.com.)

Javier Encinas joined the international unit of Partnerships UK (PUK) in 2007 and transferred to the international unit of Infrastructure UK (IUK) in 2010. Since 2007, Javier has been involved in providing advisory support to overseas governments implementing PPP policy, programs, and projects. He coordinates IUK's international training programs and is also a member of the IUK team looking at international cost comparisons for infrastructure delivery, leading the international work. Prior to joining PUK, Javier worked for Renault and for a Paris-based think tank, and undertook strategy consulting and corporate finance assignments with Citigroup and Roche. Javier holds an MBA with distinction and specialization in finance from Manchester Business School in the United Kingdom, and MA/BA degrees (*Diplôme de Grande École*) from the *Institut d'Études Politiques de Paris* (*Sciences-Po*) in France. He is fluent in English, French, and Spanish.

ABBREVIATIONS

BEE	black economic empowerment
BNDES	Banco Nacional de Desenvolvimento Econômico e Social (Brazil)
CMU	concession monitoring unit
DFI	development finance institution
EBRD	European Bank for Reconstruction and Development
EoI	expression of interest
GPOBA	Global Partnership on Output-based Aid
HRAEB	Hospital Regional de Alta Especialidad del Bajío
IALCH	Inkosi Albert Luthuli Central Hospital
IDB	Inter-American Development Bank
IFC	International Finance Corporation
KZN DoH	KwaZulu Natal Department of Health
MWC	Manila Water Company
NHAI	National Highways Authority of India
NHDP	National Highways Development Project
OBA	output-based aid
PPI	private participation in infrastructure
PPIAF	Public-Private Infrastructure Advisory Facility
PPP	public-private partnership
PPS	Projects for the Provision of Services
PQQ	prequalification questionnaire
PSC	public sector comparator
RfP	request for proposal
RfQ	request for qualification

QAIA	Queen Alia International Airport
SEEG	Societé d'Energie et d'Eau du Gabon
SEWRC	State Energy and Water Regulatory Commission
SMART	specific, measurable, achievable, realistic, and timely
TET	technical evaluation team
VfM	value for money
VGF	viability gap funding

1.

INTRODUCTION

What transforms a desirable project on a government wish list to an attractive investment opportunity in the eyes of a potential private sector partner? This guide seeks to enhance the chances of developing effective partnerships between the public and the private sectors by addressing one of the main obstacles to the effective delivery of public-private partnership (PPP) projects: having the right information on the right project for the right partners at the right time.

Data from the World Bank and the Public-Private Infrastructure Advisory Facility (PPIAF) private participation in infrastructure (PPI) project database indicate that private sector investment in infrastructure in developing economies grew steadily over the past decade (see figure 1.1).[1] By 2007 the levels had finally surpassed the peak levels seen in 1997, the end of the previous growth spurt.

However, the history of international credit flows shows that when international markets are down, emerging markets with less developed domestic sources of long-term credit can suffer disproportionately as international lenders retreat back to their own domestic markets, while those with stronger domestic markets may be less affected. The recent credit crisis, started in mid-2008, is only the most recent instance of this (see figure 1.2).

---

[1] The World Bank and PPIAF PPI project database includes some classes of projects that are not public-private partnerships as defined here, such as privatization projects or investment in sectors such as mobile telephony (see appendix A); it does not include social infrastructure PPP projects. The data also rely on investment commitments, which may turn out to be different from actual investment. Collecting consistent, reliable information on projects remains a challenge, and the data should be treated with such limitations in mind.

Figure 1.1 Investment Commitments to New and Existing Infrastructure Projects with Private Participation in Developing Countries, by Sector, 1990–2008

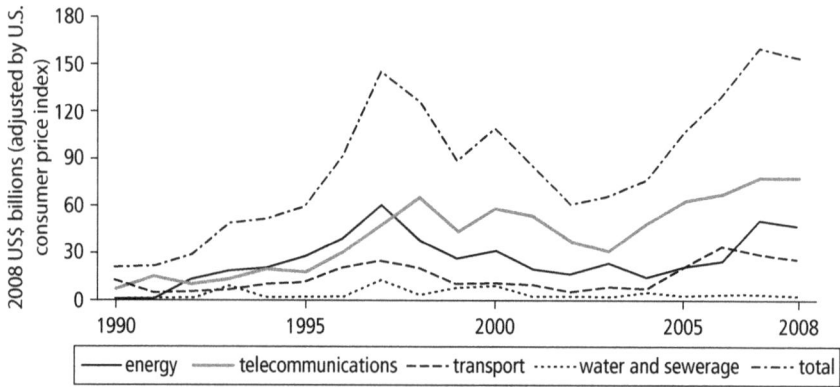

Source: World Bank and PPIAF PPI project database.

Figure 1.2 Investment Commitments to New PPI Projects Reaching Closure in Developing Countries, by Region, 1995–2009

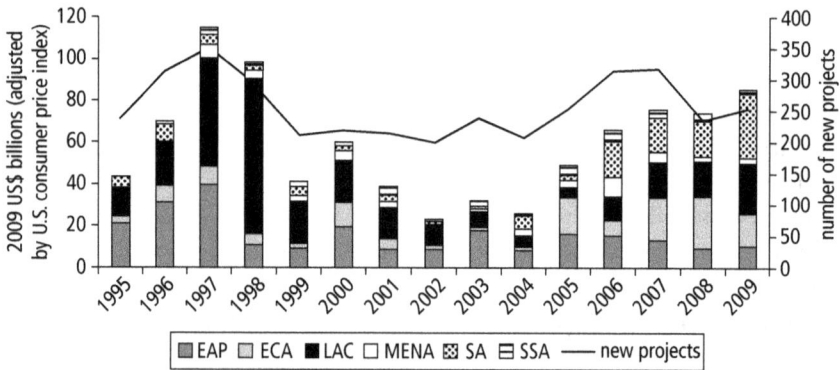

Sources: World Bank and PPIAF PPI project database and impact of the crisis on PPI database.
Note: Includes only investment commitments at financial or contractual closure; does not include additional investment in subsequent quarters. EAP = East Asia and Pacific; ECA = Eastern Europe and Central Asia; LAC = Latin America and the Caribbean; MENA = Middle East and North Africa; SA = South Asia; SSA = Sub-Saharan Africa.

Where credit availability falls, lenders then demand higher returns and more onerous terms for the risks they are being asked to take and their tolerance of risk declines. This may have an impact on whole sectors of the market: projects that rely on user demand may struggle more to raise funding than projects that are based on government payments for the availability of a service. Thus, rather than paying for the perceptions (no doubt valid) of higher risk, the challenge is to derisk the situation. Projects more likely to reach closure are characterized by strong economic and financial fundamentals, the backing of financially solid sponsors, and government support.

Over the past decade, there has also been a growing diversity of project sponsors, with firms from emerging economies such as India and China playing a more important role (von Klaudy, Sanghi, and Dellacha 2008). Despite the various crises, an unmistakable trend has been the emergence of the private sector as both a more commonplace and a more diversified player in the delivery of infrastructure services.

However, private sector participation in the financing and delivery of infrastructure services still addresses only a fraction of the demand. Differences also exist between sectors, regions, and types of projects. According to the World Bank and PPIAF PPI database, energy and transport, and to a certain extent telecommunications, have attracted larger shares of investment, while water and sewerage continue to remain challenging sectors for private investment. The data also reveal that investors have tended to favor greenfield projects over projects that rehabilitate existing assets. This would suggest that investors have become generally more cautious about the risks associated with rehabilitating existing infrastructure assets. They are also more wary about sectors that involve political and regulatory risks, especially those that involve tariff issues for end users in socially sensitive areas such as water.

Issues that affect the *supply* of well-prepared projects, rather than the *demand* for such projects, have been the main constraints to mobilizing private sector investment and delivery of infrastructure. Given the difficult environment for long-term private sector investment, the challenge will be for even better discipline in the selection and development of projects.

This guide focuses specifically on what should be done, and when, in order to prepare projects to attract the right long-term private partners, procure their involvement, and manage the partnership. This guide is not a detailed project preparation manual; rather, it seeks to provide an overview of the process and what is involved so that greater realism can be applied to this challenging task and adequate resource plans can be developed.

Role of Public-Private Partnerships

Many governments turn to the private sector to design, build, finance, and/ or operate new and existing infrastructure facilities in order to improve the delivery of services and the management of facilities hitherto provided by the public sector. Governments are attracted by the benefits of mobilizing private capital: the estimated demand for investment in public services shows that government and even donor resources cannot fill the investment gap alone, and so harnessing private capital can help to speed up the delivery of public infrastructure.

PPPs, in particular those with long-term contracts, can bring significant benefits for governments in the delivery of public services, such as the following:

- *Greater efficiency in the use of resources.* By allocating the management of risks optimally between the public and private sectors, a well-managed PPP preparation and bidding process can enable a more *efficient use of resources* over the lifetime of the asset, as the private partner has an incentive to consider the long-term implications of the costs of design and construction quality or the costs of expansion in the case of existing facilities. At the same time, the long-term nature of the contract can generate *greater certainty* (or even a reduction) in the price of service delivery, in real terms. This is especially the case for those PPPs, described more fully in chapter 2, where the public sector is purchasing a service on behalf of the taxpayer: known prices have clear value within a highly constrained public sector budgetary system, as they greatly reduce the likelihood of surprises down the line. This also ensures budgeting for proper long-term maintenance of assets, which is often omitted in traditional forms of public sector procurement to the detriment of the asset and the taxpayer.
- *Capital at risk to performance.* The explicit exposure of capital to long-term performance risk gives the private party an incentive to design and build the asset on time and within budget and to take into account the costs of longer-term maintenance and renewal. It underpins the required allocation of risks.
- *Quality assurance and scrutiny.* The PPP process usually involves a much greater level of quality assurance than the standard public procurement process as the public authority prepares its projects and engages with the market. The public authority will face scrutiny by parties outside government, such as lenders and investors, whose capital will be at risk over the long term, depending on the performance of service delivery.
- *The more open scrutiny* of the long-term commitment required of a PPP usually requires information about the true long-term risks and therefore costs to deliver the public service. This scrutiny can generate a more informed and realistic debate on project *selection* and a focus on *outputs* and even *outcomes*. Such additional quality assurance and scrutiny are often absent in conventionally procured projects.

These benefits have important implications for PPP policy even where the availability of long-term private funding is more constrained. In other words, there are some fundamental policy drivers to use PPPs even if, at times, private financing is constrained. Looking ahead, good PPP structures can endure and can simply adapt to changes in the market.

PPPs therefore can make governments think and behave in new ways that require new skills. They can be a tool for reforming procurement and public service delivery and not merely a means of leveraging private sector resources (see box 1.1). PPPs are also more than a one-off financial transaction with the private sector. As a consequence, they need to be based on firm policy foundations, a long-term political commitment, and a sound and predictable legal and regulatory environment. Sophisticated private sector partners understand this and will look for these factors when deciding whether or not to bid for a project. The other challenge for governments, especially

---

BOX 1.1

Port Concessioning and Competition in Colombia

The concession of four public ports in Colombia in the early 1990s is a good example of using PPPs to drive reform aimed at increasing competition and addressing structural problems of poor productivity and heavy labor and pension costs. Under 20-year concessions offered for four separate ports, the concessionaires were responsible for managing each port and for contracting with port operators for the use of the port facilities. New laws abolished restrictive labor laws and allowed stevedoring services to compete freely in each port. In parallel, a General Port Superintendent was established as a regulator for the concessions, a new pension fund was established to cover substantial labor retrenchment, and the former public port authority, Colpuertos, was dismantled.

As a result of these reforms, and the resulting competition between ports and of stevedoring within the ports, there was a strong increase in productivity, a decrease in the users' fees, a steady flow of revenues to government as payment for the lease of the facilities, and attractive returns to the concessionaires. With evidence of this success, further private investment was encouraged, as concessionaires started investing heavily in container cranes, and the stevedoring companies in shoreside equipment.

Source: Summary extracted from Gaviria 1998.

in emerging markets, is the fact that resources are usually less readily available for activities that lay the *foundations* for a successful PPP than for project-specific procurement activities. However, without the right policies, institutions, and processes, the transactions that follow will often fail.

Most forms of PPP involve a contractual relationship between the public and private parties (for example, a concession). The long-term nature of these contracts can create a strong long-term mutuality of interest: they differ from traditional (input-based) procurement contracts, under which the client government will often be tempted to micro-manage the decisions of project implementation and so carry much of the associated risk. Contractors seldom miss the opportunity to increase their prices, which are linked to inputs, and so this style of contract is often associated with a short-term "claims culture." Early evidence of operational contracts in more mature PPP programs shows that in many cases the parties recognize this mutuality of interest without adversely affecting the mechanisms in the formal contract that determine performance (Ipsos Mori Social Research Institute 2009).

Scope of the Guide

This guide starts with a review of the scope of public-private partnerships in chapter 2, as this is an area where interpretations can vary widely. The guide then takes a sequential look at the development of projects from first principles. Chapter 3 examines the foundation blocks for engaging with the private sector, and chapter 4 follows with an assessment of the issues relevant to project selection. Chapter 5 examines financing issues, which are especially relevant in the current environment. Chapter 6 reviews the actions involved in preparing projects for market, including how the process should be managed. The particular issue of managing advisers is examined in chapter 7, while chapter 8 looks at how the public sector should interact with the private sector during the subsequent phases of project selection and preparation, to ensure that decisions made during these phases are based on a realistic view of what the private sector can provide. The last two chapters look briefly at the issues of engagement with the private sector during the stage of competitive procurement or tender (chapter 9) and after the contract has been signed (chapter 10). While contract signature is often regarded as the conclusion of the process, the true success of the project will depend on the quality of services delivered to citizens over the life of the project. Several brief case studies are included to illustrate some of the key messages.

The proper preparation of PPP projects may appear to be daunting at first. However, breaking the task into a series of defined steps and processes

Figure 1.3   Key Phases of the Public-Private Partnership Project Process

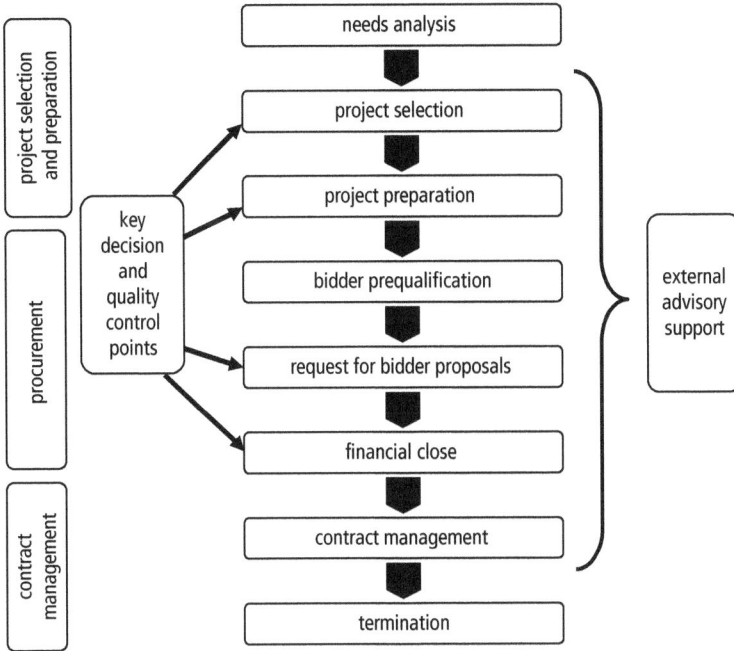

Source: Authors.

(many of which also apply to traditional public investment projects) can greatly simplify the process (see figure 1.3). Equally, the public sector cannot be expected to have all the necessary resources in-house; legal, technical, financial, environmental, and other advisers are frequently used throughout the process. The challenge is to select the right advisers and to manage them effectively.

Limits to the Guide

There are inevitable limits to the usefulness of any guide in an area as complex as PPP project development, especially where the scope of projects and the range of operating environments vary enormously. This is a guide, not a detailed set of rules. It has been prepared with the aim of setting out for public sector officials, charged with delivering infrastructure projects, a possible route to help to attract adequate private sector interest for their projects in a competitive process and a challenging environment, with a particular focus on emerging economies. Most of the statistical information focuses on basic infrastructure sectors, but the guide also includes examples and case studies from PPPs in social sectors to illustrate the possible applications of this approach. The most important task is to set realistic expectations of what is likely to be involved and to raise awareness of alternative approaches when preparing projects to attract the right private sector partner. It is important to remind the reader that this is only one aspect of the PPP process. The PPP process is not just about transactions: a PPP is a marriage, not a wedding ceremony. There are other equally important areas such as setting the policy criteria for public investment and selecting the projects to meet such criteria, not to mention the long-term management of the subsequent partnership. These areas are touched on only briefly in this guide. The following pages are intended to provide helpful general principles to inform the development of more detailed practices and approaches.

2.

DEFINING PUBLIC-PRIVATE PARTNERSHIPS

The term public-private partnership (PPP) does not have a legal meaning and can be used to describe a wide variety of arrangements involving the public and private sectors working together in some way. Policy makers have invented an ingenious array of terms to summarize what they are trying to achieve. It is therefore necessary for them to be very clear about *why* they are looking to partner with the private sector, *what* forms of PPP they have in mind, and *how* they should articulate this complex concept.

PPPs are contractual arrangements of varied nature where the two parties share rights and responsibilities during the duration of the contract. Different forms of PPPs may exist involving various combinations of public and private sector finance and exposure to project risk. The various arrangements often reflect the different appetites for risk and the role of the private party varies based on the sector and the nature of the market. This guide focuses on those PPPs that involve significant private financing because these are usually more complex to prepare and imply a greater involvement from both parties throughout the life of the project.

Privatization and Management Contracts

PPPs are often confused with privatization. There is a clear difference between these two forms of private sector engagement: privatization involves the permanent transfer of a previously publicly owned asset to the private sector, whereas a PPP necessarily involves a continuing role for the public sector as a "partner" in an ongoing relationship with the private sector.[1] Under a PPP,

---

[1] When privatization is partial rather than total, the public sector may remain involved in the firm depending on the degree of control actually transferred to the private sector.

accountability for provision of the service is clearly in the hands of the public sector, and there is a direct contractual relationship between the government and the private sector provider. With privatization, immediate accountability for providing the service may often transfer to the private provider (although *ultimately* the citizen may hold government accountable): if the telephone in a privatized telecommunications utility does not work, the citizen will normally complain to the private provider, but if a PPP hospital is closed, the citizen will still hold the government immediately accountable. These distinctions can be important when governments seek to engage public understanding of and support for PPPs and begin to identify the skills and processes needed for the very different PPP processes. Some governments have deliberately sought to brand their PPP programs to distinguish them directly from privatization and in some cases even from previous forms of concessioning. In Mexico, for example, certain PPP projects are referred to as projects for the provision of services (PPS), and in Peru PPP projects have been branded in the legal framework as co-financed concessions.

Other forms of private sector involvement may entail shorter-term management contracts or (longer-term) lease or *affermage* arrangements with limited private sector investment. Management of rural roads and water and sewerage projects often use this approach. Urban water utilities in developing countries, for example, may involve leases or *affermage* contracts, where the private sector enters into a long-term arrangement with the public authority to operate and maintain a facility and implement an investment program in the utility, although the public sector retains the responsibility for financing the investment. These projects share some common characteristics with the capital-intensive PPPs discussed in this guide, and many of the steps described may be equally applicable to preparing such projects and attracting good operators. However, the transfer of risks to the private sector is more limited, with implications for the incentives and nature of the partnership. In particular, while the private party's profit may be at risk under a management contract, only limited private sector capital is at stake, and therefore important disciplinary mechanisms found in capital-intensive PPPs, such as the lenders' due diligence and subsequent exposure of capital investment to performance risk, are absent or at least considerably reduced.

Small Private Providers of Infrastructure Services

PPPs are not necessarily confined to the involvement of large players, either foreign or domestic, and a growing number of arrangements involve relatively small-scale domestic providers of services. Again, many of the disciplinary mechanisms described in this guide will apply, but these may require further approaches not covered here. Examples of such projects include isolated electricity grids operated by local distribution companies or the provision of water by small independent providers, as is found in Paraguay ("los Aguateros"). In many cases, though not all, these arrangements may be more akin to management contracts involving only relatively modest amounts of private capital.

User-Fee and Availability-Based Public-Private Partnerships

This guide focuses primarily on those PPPs that arrange for a private party to provide public infrastructure under a long-term *contract* with a public sector body.[2] Under such an arrangement, the private sector party usually agrees to undertake the following:

- Design and build, expand, or upgrade the public sector infrastructure
- Assume substantial financial, technical, and operational risks
- Receive a financial return through payments over the life of the contract from users, from the public sector, or from a combination of the two
- Usually return the infrastructure to public sector ownership at the end of the contract.

Terms such as BOT (build, operate, and transfer) and DBFO (design, build, finance, and operate) are often used to describe such schemes. Such terms also apply to long-term concessions where the private sector is responsible for the operation, maintenance, and expansion of existing assets. When the underlying asset is not returned to the public sector, it is sometimes referred to as a BOO (build, own, and operate) contract, and the procedures to select, prepare, and bid these types of projects are usually no different. Each sector may have its own particular issues, but these approaches can apply across a wide range of infrastructure provision. Whether in power generation, the building and maintenance of roads, or the provision of schools or hospitals, the broad nature of the PPP is determined by what rights, obligations, and risks are assumed by the public or private parties within the partnership. In this regard, these forms of PPP can be broadly broken down into two further categories: user-fee and availability-based PPPs. In some countries (Brazil, for example), separate PPP laws and even institutions may be established for different forms of PPP.

User-Fee PPPs

In a user-fee PPP, a public authority grants a private party the right to design, build (or refurbish or expand), maintain, operate, and finance an infrastructure asset owned by the public sector. Often described as a concession agreement, the user-fee PPP contract is for a fixed period, say 25–30

---

[2] Referred to in this guide as the "public authority," this body may be a central, regional, or local government, an autonomous public body such as a roads agency, or a public enterprise.

years, after which responsibility for operation reverts to the public authority. The private party recoups its investment, operating, and financing costs and its profit by charging members of the public a user fee (for example, a road toll). Thus a key feature is that the private party is usually allocated the risk of demand for use of the asset, in addition to the risks of design, finance, construction, and operation. However, demand risk may be allocated in various ways: for example, the public authority may share the risk by underwriting a minimum level of usage, and, therefore, the public sector may also be involved in making payments to the private sector under certain circumstances. (It may also do so in the form of a subsidy for the capital costs. In other cases, it may extend the concession contract period to enable the private party to collect user fees over a longer period.) The level of user charges may be prescribed in the PPP concession agreement itself, by a regulator (implementing a tariff adjustment mechanism set out in the legislation or in the concession agreement), or even by the concessionaire. Typical examples of these types of PPP include toll roads, railways, urban transport schemes, ports, airports, and even the provision of power, water, gas distribution, and telecommunications. The competence and autonomy of a regulator or of a monitoring entity, where it is required, are crucial features of these forms of PPP.

Availability-Based PPPs

The other main form of PPP has some similarities with user-fee PPPs, in that it also involves a private party designing, financing, building or rebuilding, and subsequently operating and maintaining the necessary infrastructure. However, in this case, the public authority—not the end users—makes payments to the private party. These payments are usually made as, when, and to the extent that a service (not an asset) is made *available*.[3] Hence the demand or usage risk usually remains with the public authority. This form of PPP has important implications for the detail required to define, monitor, and pay for the service by the public sector; the implications for affordability for the public sector; and the procurement methodology used.

The availability-based PPP had its genesis in power purchase agreements used in independent power producer projects (IPPs), where the power offtaker was a public authority. In such projects, private investors typically build a power generation plant and contract to sell the electricity generated to a publicly owned power utility (or to a private distribution company, although in this case it would not be a PPP, as both parties are private).

---

[3] A hybrid of the user-fee (demand risk) and availability-based PPP is the use of "shadow tolls" in PPP road projects: here payment is made by the public sector, based on usage by drivers.

The public authority assumes part or all of the demand risk and makes a minimum payment for a service, in this case the availability (or capacity) of the power plant, whether or not part or all of its output (energy) is actually required—in effect a form of "take-or-pay contract." Further payments are usually made for usage, to cover at least the cost of fuel for the plant, but also in some cases for the payment of additional energy if and when it is actually delivered.

The power purchase agreement structure can be used for any kind of "process plant" project, such as the generation of electricity from gas-fired plants, the transportation of gas or oil through pipelines, and the operation of waste treatment plants.

A further development of the power purchase agreement structure is also used in social infrastructure projects, such as schools, hospitals, prisons, or government buildings, as well as in other projects that are not "self-funding," such as rural roads. Such PPPs are used where *accommodation* is provided or where *equipment* or a *system* is made available. In all these cases, payments are again generally based on the availability of the accommodation facility, equipment, or system to a defined standard and not on the volume of usage. The mechanism that determines the level of payment for the service is usually set out in considerable detail in the project agreement itself, and, accordingly, the role of a regulator may be much less extensive or even nonexistent.

Where the requirement can be well defined and is unlikely to vary significantly over the life of the agreement, governments have found these types of PPPs to be very effective in ensuring that public facilities are delivered on time and on budget, are properly maintained, and are able to deliver public services in the context of constrained resources. The United Kingdom pioneered the use of this form of PPP for the provision of social infrastructure (known as the Private Finance Initiative [PFI] Program), and many other countries, such as Australia, Brazil, Canada, Japan, the Republic of Korea, Mexico, and South Africa, are using this approach.

For the purposes of this guide, these types of PPPs are called "availability-based PPPs." In some countries, these forms of PPPs are referred to as annuity schemes. However, if an annuity is paid *irrespective* of performance (a crucial element of a PPP contract), these schemes are just another form of government borrowing and fall outside the scope of PPPs as discussed in this guide.

Whether to pursue a user-fee or an availability-based PPP is both a policy decision and a reflection of who is best placed to pay for the service. The affordability of availability-based PPPs is likely to be an issue in some developing countries, because such projects require public resources and do not themselves raise revenue through user-payment mechanisms. Availability-based PPPs also require that the long-term payment obligations of the government are acceptable to investors, especially since such payments may rely on multiannual budget approvals. However, user-fee PPPs also present their own challenges with regard to demand risk and user affordability (see Harris and Patrap 2008 on how these risks may be higher in some sectors and play a role in the cancellation of projects). Faced with these challenges, the solution in a particular situation may involve blending user fees and public service charges and, in some cases, tailoring overseas development assistance into longer-term, performance-based contracting support. These mechanisms can often create much more stable projects, as demand risk—a common cause of project failure—is shared. On the funding side, the solution may also involve mixing different forms of finance and funding support (as is happening even in mature PPP markets in the current climate). These issues are discussed further in this guide. In many markets, particularly those with availability-based schemes, PPPs are now seen as a method of procuring public services, not just as a means of financing infrastructure. Looked at in this light, other forms of partnership are also developing to provide greater flexibility (although they often are more complex). These may involve partnerships to manage whole programs of investment and service delivery (rather than individual projects), particularly in cases where the timing or nature of future requirements may vary, but where there are still significant benefits to sharing risk and taking a strategic approach with a private sector partner. The United Kingdom adopted this approach for some of its primary health care and schools infrastructure under which the private and public sectors become partners to deliver a whole program of infrastructure investment within a region over a defined period, with the identification and timing of delivery of many of the individual facilities taking place over the life of the program. This guide does not cover these forms of partnership, but it is important to be aware that increasing and varied forms of PPPs are emerging around the world.

3.

SETTING THE FRAMEWORK

An effective public-private partnership (PPP) framework can help to ensure a strong private sector response. This involves establishing a clear rationale for PPP policy, backed by well-thought-out legal, regulatory, and investment frameworks. In addition, a strong institutional platform is required to help shape and deliver policy, prepare and procure the project outputs, and manage or regulate the associated project agreements. All this needs to be broadcast to potential investors from the highest authority. It is vital that potential investors (and indeed the public administration itself) see ownership of the framework at this level.

In countries where public sector processes and institutional capacity are weak, managing the relatively complex PPP process is especially challenging and should not be underestimated. Governments should seek to ensure that the early-stage activities are sufficiently resourced.

Public sector resources are often made available only at the later stages of project preparation, usually at or near the tendering or procurement phase. Resources are usually much less readily available at the early stages of program or project preparation. This is often because the outcomes are less well defined or certain at this stage. However, investing time and effort up-front in laying the right foundations is crucial to the success of a PPP program and the projects involved. It may also be said that each dollar of resource and week of time spent in sound project preparation will save multiples of these precious resources in the eventual successful delivery of the project.

Policy Rationale

Establishing a clear policy framework helps both the public and the private sectors to understand the core rationale for PPPs and how the public sector will go about making them happen. PPPs are difficult to deliver in an unstable policy environment. When assessing a PPP market, the private sector expects to see a PPP policy that sets out the following:

- The public policy rationale for using PPPs
- The guidelines that the public sector will use to select, prepare, and procure PPP projects in a *consistent* way
- The determination of who approves what and when throughout the process of project selection, preparation, and procurement
- The process of resolving disputes (often set out in legislation or in sector regulations, but often—in more detail—in the contract itself)
- The arrangements for monitoring the contract after it has been signed.

Private sector firms will want to know what is involved in the bid process to assess how much it will cost to prepare and submit a bid, and to decide whether it is worth their while to participate in the process. They will want to know whether and when detailed designs will have to be developed; how long the bidding process will take; how workable, competitive, and transparent it will be; how the public authority will manage the partnership in the long term; what the impact of sector regulation, if any, will be on their contract; how the contract work will be supervised; and, above all, how committed the government is to the project. The more transparent are the objectives, targets, and consequences of the PPP, the more effective the partnership will be.

Governments should expect to establish a clear evaluation and process map that sets out the following: key decision points along the process, timelines, criteria for project selection and eligibility, and principles or criteria for evaluating bids.

By way of example, South Africa's Public Finance Management Act regulates and sets out the responsibilities to ensure efficient and effective government financial management. Under this act, Treasury Regulation 16 specifies the required approvals and responsibilities. Detailed guidance, in the form of a PPP manual, has been developed to cover the range of processes involved.[1]

Legal and Regulatory Framework

Private sector investors will always examine the legal and regulatory framework and its ability to ensure the effectiveness of long-term PPP contracts. Legislation may be needed to allow a private sector company to charge and

---

[1] See http://www.treasury.gov.za/legislation/PFMA/default.aspx and http://www.treasury.gov.za/legislation/PFMA/act.pdf.

collect user fees. Specific laws may also be required to allow the public sector to contract with private bodies for the delivery of services hitherto provided only by the state. For example, considerable preparation was necessary to adopt important reforms to allow private participation in the provision of water and electricity services in Gabon (see the case study at the end of this chapter). For user-fee PPPs, private investors will also seek clarity about the government's commitment to adopt a price policy that will ensure the financial viability of the contract (accompanied by the adoption of transparent subsidies if the government decides that not all consumers can afford to pay cost-recovery tariffs). Furthermore, regulatory frameworks may be needed in many of the infrastructure sectors where PPPs are most likely to be used. In some cases, sectors may be undergoing reforms, and the signature of the contract may precede the adoption of a broader sectoral framework. When the regulatory framework and institutions are already in place, private sector investors will always assess features such as the technical capacity and autonomy of the regulators, the predictability of the decisions, and the transparency of the processes. The existence of clear monitoring mechanisms with which to supervise the project after it has been signed is also important because it increases predictability and transparency for all parties involved. In sum, governments need to prepare the ground for private sector participation by developing an appropriate legal, regulatory, institutional, and contractual framework.

The following key questions regarding the legal and regulatory framework are likely to be asked by both potential investors and their lenders:

- Are unsolicited proposals permitted, and, if so, how will they be treated?
- How fair and transparent is the bidding process likely to be?
- Does the public sector have a robust, forward-planning program and allocation process to ensure that government payments can be made when due, such as obligations against future budgets?
- What is the legal capacity of the public sector party to enter into and ensure that it will meet these long-term payment commitments, and is there a risk that such obligations could be transferred to a body without such capacity?
- Is combined procurement of construction and long-term operation and maintenance permitted (or do these phases have to be procured under separate contracts)?
- Does the public sector contracting party have the legal power to transfer the provision of the public service to a private sector party?
- Are there sector regulations and regulatory institutions that oversee the sector where the PPP will take place? If so, what is the hierarchical relation

between those sector regulations and the content of a particular contract, and are they consistent?

- If a broader regulatory framework is adopted for the sector after a contract has been signed, what happens to the contract? Is there a transition path for harmonizing the contract with the regulations?
- What is the role of the regulator, if any, in supervising the contract during implementation, and how much discretion does the regulator have (Bakovic, Tenenbaum, and Woolf 2003)?
- How will end-user tariffs or availability tariffs be set?
- What are the investors' rights if a contract is terminated early? What are the government's rights if the investor walks away?
- How will local accounting regulations affect the distribution of profits, and how will repatriation of profits be treated for foreign investors?
- What restrictions, if any, will there be on the use of qualified expatriate personnel?
- What are the lenders' rights (for example, the lenders' ability to take over management of the asset when enforcing their security) in the event of borrower default?
- How will contract disputes be resolved and enforced, and what rights and obligations are required of the parties if the project does not go according to plan?
- How will payments be taxed under the project (for example, sales or value added taxes on construction costs or service payments)?
- What forms of government support are likely to be available for certain risks (for example, minimum-traffic guarantees on a toll road)?
- How will changes to the contract be handled, and what compensation mechanisms will be used?
- Who will bear the risk of a change of law, and what is the likelihood of such changes (for example, the imposition of a new withholding tax)?

The extent to which these issues are covered in general administrative law, in sector regulations, or in specific provisions in the PPP contract itself depends on the legal system.[2] It may also depend on whether the government

---

[2] In developed countries, two broad models of regulation have emerged: regulation by an "independent regulator" or "regulation by contract." However, the distinction is only approximate, because there are PPPs without regulators (for instance, in roads or hospitals), which rely solely on the content of the contract, and, even where there are independent regulators, PPP transactions always entail the signature of a binding contract. Furthermore, in developing countries, this sharp distinction is often of limited empirical relevance because they often have adopted hybrid regulatory models that combine elements of the two approaches (Brown, Stern, and Tenenbaum 2006).

is already engaged in an overall reform of the sector—which often includes a PPP program—and has developed regulatory frameworks for the sector. Alternatively, there can be countries where the opportunity of undertaking one or various PPP transactions arises before a legal and regulatory framework is in place. In that case, these pioneering transactions—if well structured—could constitute the first steps in building a broader framework, as the specific provisions could be incorporated within the broader framework. It is also true that, whereas specific circumstances may vary and should be taken into consideration, countries could also benefit from adopting legal and regulatory solutions used in markets with successfully operating PPP programs, as the private sector is already familiar with these approaches.[3]

There is often a *balance* to be struck between a fixed legal and regulatory framework and a flexible one capable of responding to developments in best practice over time. In general, investors have a strong preference for certainty, detail, and clarity in the legislative framework, so long as it is a good framework. However, as a note of caution, highly detailed PPP legislation or sector legislation has sometimes been developed from an early stage of a PPP program without input from the experience of actual projects (functioning either domestically or internationally). This legislation has sometimes proved to be unworkable and difficult to change. It may sometimes be preferable to set out *core principles* (based on international best practice) in framework legislation and to use administrative rules or regulations to set out more *detailed rules* that may respond, in a logical, consistent, and consultative way, to inevitable changes in policy and the market (so long as this does not lead to a panoply of conflicting and arbitrary rules and regulations). That said, the experience in developing countries with weak institutions and scarce institutional capacity has shown that, in some cases, leaving too much discretion to design and modify specific rules and regulations may lead to inefficient results, because the government officials in charge do not have the technical expertise to elaborate them or to supervise appropriately the external consultants who may advise them. Therefore, there may be a case in those circumstances for having less flexibility and instead establishing clear but stable rules that would benefit from the growing body of international experiences in regulating infrastructure sectors and implementing PPP programs (Eberhard 2007, 2008; Shugart and Alexander 2009).

---

[3] For more information on contracts, laws, and regulations for PPPs in infrastructure, visit the Web site of the PPP Infrastructure Resource Center for Contracts, Laws, and Regulations: http://www.worldbank.org/pppiresource.

It is important to remember that private finance—both debt providers and equity investors—will require contractual and, if applicable, regulatory certainty as a precondition of participation in a PPP in which their capital is exposed to risk (which is normally the case). Governments sometimes prepare standardized or model project agreements that encapsulate the obligations of the public and private parties in great detail, in effect reflecting the allocation of risks between the two parties. This may take the form of mandated contracts that are not open for negotiation (an approach currently used, for example, in India), or it may be a more exegetic document—that is, a document that sets out and explains core principles with only certain key terms and mandatory conditions (the U.K. government takes this approach with its standardized form of Private Finance Initiative contract). At the other extreme, contracts may be negotiated separately for each project. The latter approach can lead to greater time and expense and the likelihood that the rights and obligations, and hence risk allocation, may vary between contracts more than they need: it could also reduce the transparency of the process and leave excessive room for ad hoc negotiations for lack of a clear framework of reference. Many risk allocation issues will, in fact, be similar between projects, and it is preferable for the public sector to have a consistent approach and a clear framework for contracting as well as soliciting and evaluating bids from interested investors and operators. Standardization of some form also enables the public sector to negotiate as a whole—and therefore more effectively—on key issues and to ensure a level of consistency across contracts. At the same time, standardized contracts, while locking in key terms, can also lock out key innovations and modifications required due to changes in the market, policy, or sector-specific issues, so having a disciplined central process for review and revision from time to time is also important.

There is a balance to be struck between the advantages and limitations of giving greater flexibility to the bidders or operators, which will often depend on the sector where they operate and the nature of the contract. The balance will also depend on the maturity of the PPP program in a given country or sector. The costs of preparing and managing a PPP project will have a direct impact on the benefits that the PPP option can offer as an alternative. Introducing standard guidance and sector-specific model contracts can help to improve such value for money, as those measures can be used to identify lessons from closed projects of relevance to subsequent projects. It can also promote a common understanding of the main risks encountered in PPP projects and reduce the period and costs of negotiations—that is, reduce the transaction costs for delivering a PPP project and improve the quality of contracts. However, using standardized contracts to transfer experience from earlier to later deals is harder to achieve at the outset of a PPP program or before some pathfinder projects have been undertaken; therefore, an adequate team of advisers with international experience and a full understanding of the legal framework can play an important role. It may be a mistake to standardize (mandate) contracts before enough experience has been accumulated and good practices have been circulated among the government entities involved in preparing and bidding PPPs. At the same time, waiting too long to adopt standardized contracts may not be optimum, as the public sector would be giving up the advantages that some standardization can provide.

Wider procurement law may also have a bearing. In many countries, particularly in Latin America, procurement law and jurisprudence, and hence new PPP legislation, will most likely require the procurement authority to provide a model contract to bidders that will not be open for negotiation once the procurement process has been launched or after bidders have been short listed. In such cases, where structured dialogue with bidders is limited or prohibited, having a consultation process prior to the bidding process will be of paramount importance if the public sector wants to take into account private sector innovations and requirements. In these countries detailed project preparation needs to be conducted even earlier. The detailed project scoping, definition of outputs, identification and allocation of risks, and market sounding, all of which are discussed later in this guide, need to be carried out prior to launching the bidding process and before the views of the private party in a competitive situation are known. The role of advisers in developing a sensible risk matrix will therefore be of particular importance, as will the use of guidance and model agreements, calling for the existence of a strong and capable PPP unit (see figure 3.1). Once the contract is signed, it is also generally good practice, and in the interests of transparency, to make the contract available to the public by, for example, publishing the contract on the PPP unit's Web site (subject to any commercially sensitive issues).

Investment Framework

PPP programs often start with one-off "pathfinder" projects that deliver experience and build confidence in the ability of government to develop programs later. In many countries, there may simply be only one or two projects in a sector, too few to constitute a program.

Wherever possible, an infrastructure plan or priority list is a good way for a government to present its investment plans to the private sector and to demonstrate top-level political commitment. Investment plans must be presented carefully and in the proper context so that they are not perceived simply as a wish list of projects, lacking credibility and coherence.

Figure 3.1 Relationship between When to Standardize Contract Terms and Benefits from the Project

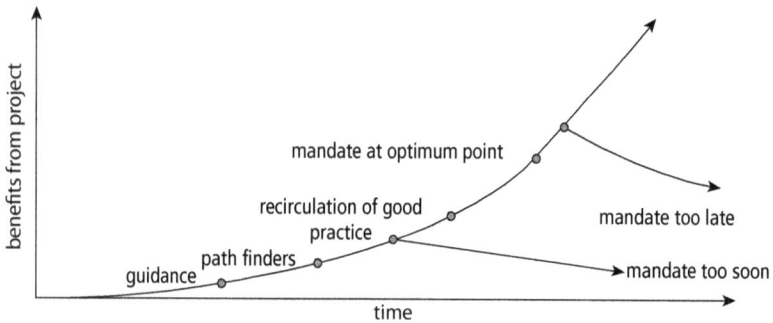

Source: Authors.

High-quality plans generally do not commit to using the PPP process for the entire program, but instead set out the level of investment required, the links between private and public investment, and the areas within the plan where government expects PPPs to play a role. The plan developed by the state government of Minas Gerais in Brazil is a good example of this approach.[4]

Also, wherever the opportunity arises, it makes sense to develop *programs*, that is, a series of PPP projects in specific sectors, as the benefits of replicability for both the costs and the quality of the PPP process can be significant for both the public and the private sectors. The National Highways Development Program in India, described in chapter 6, is an example of this approach.

Well-prepared investment plans also help the private sector to understand the general environment for individual projects. A port project may make little commercial sense unless, for example, there is connecting rail transport infrastructure or reforms in transit and customs clearance.

The other useful role of investment plans, and the project pipelines that these may set out, is to encourage more bids from high-quality investors: given the costs of bid preparation, investors are more likely to take an interest in a program than in a one-off project. In a program with a series of bids, they will have more than one chance to submit a winning bid and can spread some of the general costs of bid preparation over the series.

---

[4] For a description of the PPP program in Minas Gerais, including an update on the projects implemented and under preparation, see www.ppp.mg.gov.br.

When setting the framework for PPPs, governments should also consider what they want the shape of the supply market to look like in the long run, as they can take actions early on in the development of a program to influence this. A strategy, for example, may be to guide and encourage the development of suppliers as long-term public service providers by setting out early on what good governance of such providers might look like and by using publicized league tables to encourage visible benchmarking between suppliers.

Implementation Framework

While many governments understand the need for a sound policy rationale and for strong legal and investment frameworks, investors also want assurances that *governments have the personnel* capable of managing the PPP process and that policy makers and the parties implementing projects have a realistic understanding of the complexity of PPP projects. Public procurement authorities often fail to appreciate the significant differences between PPPs and traditional forms of procurement and the implications of these differences for the level of resources, the unique skills, the output-based nature of the contracts, and the new processes and institutions required. Indeed, implementing a PPP program may often lead to fundamental changes in the way a public authority perceives its role and the way it goes about its business.

Subsequent chapters discuss the frameworks for decision making or "governance" of individual projects and how the rules relating to the development, construction, financing, and operation of PPPs are made. However, it is important to emphasize here that for PPP programs to be managed successfully, governments need to perform several specialized functions, for which they may not always be well equipped. In their study, Sanghi, Sundakov, and Hankinson (2007) identify the following functions:

- Setting PPP policies and strategies
- Originating and identifying projects
- Analyzing individual projects
- Managing transactions
- Managing, monitoring, and enforcing contracts.

When governments are unable to undertake these functions efficiently, because of lack of expertise or other constraints, various institutional solutions exist to implement these functions: each one can be performed by a line agency or by a coordinating agency (such as a cabinet office), a specialized PPP unit, or suitably managed external consultants, who can assist the various government entities involved in the PPP process. As Sanghi, Sundakov, and

Hankinson (2007) point out, if governments decide to create a PPP unit, it is important to give these units a clear and specific mandate and to grant them decision-making power, rather than only an advisory role. See box 3.1 for some of the lessons pertaining to the appropriate design and use of PPP units.

BOX 3.1

Lessons

The qualitative assessment of eight PPP units in various developing and developed countries points to some lessons with regard to the appropriate design and use of PPP units and some reasons for the positive correlation between successful PPP programs and the use of PPP units.

- *Less effective governments tend to have less effective PPP units.* Lack of political commitment to advance a PPP program or lack of transparency and coordination within government agencies will reduce the chances of success for a PPP unit. Even with a good design, a PPP unit is unlikely to be effective in such an environment.
- *Without high-level political support for the PPP program, a PPP unit most likely will fail.*
- *Relatively successful PPP units directly target specific government failures.* A clear focus on responding to particular government failures is essential to ensuring the success of the institutional solution selected.
- *The authority of a PPP unit must match what it is expected to achieve.* If a PPP unit is expected to provide quality control or assurance, it needs the authority to stop or alter a PPP that it perceives to be poorly designed. However, this executive power must be coupled with a mandate to promote good PPPs, or the unit may simply wield a veto without adding value.
- *A PPP unit's location in the government is among the most important design features,* because of the importance of interagency coordination and political support for a PPP unit's objectives. In a parliamentary system, a PPP unit is most likely to be effective if located in a strong ministry of finance or treasury. In nonparliamentary systems, such as the presidential system of the Philippines and many Latin American countries, the best location for a PPP unit is less clear. In a country with a strong planning or economic policy coordination agency, that agency might make a natural home for a PPP unit.

Source: Sanghi, Sundakov, and Hankinson 2007.

A characteristic of successful PPP units is also the capacity to understand both how government processes and administration work and how the market works, based on people with strong commercial experience. This, in turn, implies adequate resourcing to attract and retain this combination of skills and strong commitment by government to its success.

The PPP unit is generally not the public body tendering the contract (that is, it is not the contracting authority). This is the responsibility of the central, regional, or municipal government body that is sponsoring the project and that holds (or will hold) the requisite budgets for the project's procurement and long-term realization. A PPP unit, therefore, usually only plays a *supporting* role: it helps the public authority to prepare the project and, where necessary, to select and manage specialist advisers; in addition, it ensures that the project fits into the overall PPP policy framework. A PPP unit may also play a role in project *approval* and *quality assurance* throughout project development. Potential conflicts of interest between these roles can be resolved by making decisions outside the unit, even when a decision is supported by the unit's evaluation. An important principle, however, is that, in developing operational rules and processes, government must also create mechanisms to help the public authority to follow the rules. Nevertheless, balancing the roles of project support and approval is often difficult, as it requires achieving the right level of engagement between the unit and the project team. This calls for high-quality, credible staff led by someone who commands respect across government and the market and enjoys strong political support at senior levels. In cases where the program is sufficiently large, a sector-focused unit may also be found within the line ministry itself (or within a department of the regional government, as the case might be).

The importance of having a competent PPP unit that is staffed with highly qualified individuals able to work across government cannot be overemphasized, if a successful PPP program is to be delivered. Yet resourcing a PPP unit is often one of the most difficult challenges for governments at the early stages of program development.

PPP units are typically found at the central government level, the regional government level, or both. Large-city authorities may also have their own units. This largely reflects the size and structure of government and the extent to which investment decision-making powers are devolved— examples of regional PPP units can be found in Australia, Brazil, Canada, Germany, India, Mexico, and the United Kingdom to name a few. Wherever possible, the market, which does not usually recognize the "artificial impediments" of state boundaries, will generally respond better to wider, more consistent, approaches. Therefore, the role of a central or federal government unit is important to support these regional units, ensure that there is consistency of approach, and enable the sharing of best-practice information and lessons learned. Clearly, the size of the program also drives the need for a unit: it makes little sense to establish a fully resourced additional unit at a line ministry or regional government level if only a few projects are contemplated. However, even if modest in scale, when the program is being delivered mostly through municipal authorities (unaccustomed to large, complex projects), the challenge of building the public sector's technical capacity to manage the procurements and ongoing contracts is much greater. Some countries, such as the United Kingdom, have established agencies that provide support to municipal authorities across wider regions and work closely with the central PPP agency to address this issue.

As an example at the other end of the scale, the European Investment Bank has established a PPP center of excellence that serves as an active platform of support for the national and regional PPP units across the European Union. This is effectively a public sector membership club for PPP units designed to research issues of common interest and facilitate sharing of knowledge on topical issues. Other regional development finance institutions (DFIs) could potentially play an important role in this regard: the World Bank, the Public-Private Infrastructure Advisory Facility (PPIAF), and other multilateral organizations are currently looking to develop a more extensive bank of PPP management tools and guidance.

Equally, the importance of reusing or retaining the experience of public officers who have been through a PPP transaction is often poorly recognized, as individuals return to their previous functions or depart for the private sector. The experience of these officers is invaluable to the public sector as well as to the private sector, which takes considerable comfort from working with public officials who have been through the process before.

Summary

In summary, time and effort must be spent laying the foundations for successful PPPs, in particular to accomplish the following:

- Establish and clarify the policy framework, as the private sector needs to understand the drivers that lie behind the projects.
- Establish a clear legal and regulatory framework, as PPPs depend heavily on contracts that are effective and enforceable.
- Ensure consistency, as well as clarity, of the policy and legal framework, which reduces the uncertainty for investors.
- Use legal terms and approaches, where possible, that are familiar to the international private sector, if they are to be sought as partners.

- Draw up investment plans, which can be useful to demonstrate high-level political support, to indicate the potential flow of future projects, and to explain how projects fit together within the context of national or regional economic plans.
- Avoid sending out wish lists of disconnected projects that are not part of a coherent program.
- Establish a clear PPP process map, including quality assurance and approvals processes.
- Adopt the appropriate institutional solution, so that governments can effectively perform the specialized functions needed to manage successful PPP programs. When creating a PPP unit, ensure that it has the relevant commercial and legal skills needed to be a key source of support for policy makers and public bodies developing and sponsoring projects. (Taking these crucial steps will send a powerful message of consistency and credibility to the private sector about the public sector's competence and seriousness of intent.)
- Capitalize on the experience of others who have managed the process, as the private sector takes considerable comfort from working with public officials who have been through the process before.

Case Study: Water and Electricity Services Provision in Gabon

Project:	Water and electricity services provision in Gabon
Description:	20-year concession for the production, transport, and distribution of both water and electricity in Gabon; the contract can be extended for several periods based on an addendum to the contract
Financial close:	July 1997
Capital value:	US$135 million
Consortium:	Societé d'Energie et d'Eau du Gabon, comprising Vivendi Water (51 percent) and local shareholders (49 percent). The 49 percent sale of shares through a public offer was the first of its kind in Gabon. Employees were able to buy up to 5 percent of the shares.

The first contract to involve private sector participation in Africa in the water sector was awarded in 1960. To date, 27 such contracts have been signed. However, this politically sensitive sector remains one of the least popular for private investment. Nevertheless, it is possible to find successful projects in the sector. According to a report commissioned by the World Bank and the PPIAF (2002), the contract for the management of water and electricity utilities in Gabon was a relative success, thanks to the strong political commitment on the part of the government, the undertaking of essential reforms prior to the transaction, such as legal reform and tariff reform, and the restructuring of Societé d'Energie et d'Eau du Gabon (SEEG) before the transaction, so that a good social climate was preserved throughout the PPP process.[5]

In July 1997, a 20-year concession contract for the provision of both water and electricity services was signed between the government of Gabon and SEEG, which is majority-owned by Vivendi Water, a large multinational utility company. SEEG grew out of private municipal companies that provided water and electricity services in the two main urban centers, Libreville and Port-Gentil, which together comprise half the country's total population.

---

[5] While the restructuring of SEEG by the government eliminated 600 workers between 1989 and 1997, when the contract was signed, Vivendi committed to maintaining the number of employees at 90 percent of the level at the beginning of the concession (1,355 employees). See World Bank and PPIAF (2002, 12).

Extensive preparation was necessary to allow important reforms, such as the definition of a legal framework, the increase of tariffs to levels reflecting costs, and the reduction of staff. This began as early as 1989. By 1993, three laws were passed to establish the legal framework for both water and electricity sectors, while the tariff structure was reformed in 1997. This reform consisted of simplifying the tariff structure in order to eliminate all special tariffs that had been awarded to various social and professional categories. Medium-voltage electricity tariffs moved very close to their economic levels (with an increase in medium-voltage tariffs in isolated centers, to reflect the high costs of isolated thermal production), whereas the cross-subsidies between water and electricity remained in place. Once the groundwork had been laid, the transaction proceeded smoothly and transparently. Vivendi won the project on the basis of a proposed 17.25 percent reduction in the price of water and electricity services. To allow for maximum transparency, the opening of the financial bids was done publicly, and negotiations following the selection of bidders were limited to a minimum (World Bank and PPIAF 2002, 12).

This contract was the first "real" output-driven water concession in Africa: it defined investment obligations and set coverage targets for the private sector provider. For instance, the contract obliged SEEG to invest a minimum of US$135 million in rehabilitation (60 percent in water) and set coverage targets for expanding service to previously unconnected rural areas. SEEG's electricity business, particularly electricity revenues from the two main towns, cross-subsidized the less developed water business. SEEG informally committed to investing another US$130 million over the life of the contract to improve performance and coverage of the network. Although no separate dedicated regulatory body was set up, a government department within the Ministry of Water and Electricity assumed the regulatory and monitoring functions of the concession.

Nevertheless, some aspects of the contract remained undefined at award, particularly those concerning quality standards. When the government entered the contract, it lacked key information to define those standards. Rather than delaying the transaction, it took a progressive approach to contracting and decided to set aside a transition period of two and a half years, during which these aspects would be negotiated between the parties. Five years down the line, many of the elements had yet to be agreed, and important regulatory tools were still being prepared or negotiated.

The World Bank and PPIAF (2002) report that the private operator had, in the first five years, "performed well in its existing service areas, often exceeding targets, but less progress had been made in more isolated areas." The report continues, "SEEG has posted good profits since the start of its operations, paying shareholders a 20 percent dividend per share in 2000. The coverage targets, with penalties for non-achievement, have provided effective incentives for quickly increasing network density in newly served areas. The multi-utility service provision has allowed cost reduction through sharing of resources, particularly at the headquarter level. Cross-subsidization has also been effective in getting 60 percent of investment into the water sector, which only accounts for 15 percent of SEEG's turnover."

At the same time, the delays in establishing regulatory and monitoring tools to enforce quality have resulted in some skepticism on the part of the conceding authority on the reality of the improvements mentioned above, "because it is very difficult to assess the overall efficiency of the company and the potential for further improvements." In fact, the World Bank and PPIAF report notes, "Installing monitoring systems together with an adequate analytical accounting system and computer systems remains one of the major challenges for the concessionaire, who was at the time when the report was written in the process of installing these systems, if only as a way of improving its own management."

Key lessons from this project are the following:

- Government provided strong policy support to the project since its conception.
- Government prepared the ground for private sector participation by developing an appropriate legal, institutional, and contractual framework and by putting in place an appropriate pricing policy.
- Government preserved a good social climate throughout processing of the transaction by completing the restructuring of SEEG prior to the operation.
- The contract defined the investment obligations and set coverage targets for the consortium.
- The experience in this case shows that if some contractual clauses are to be negotiated during the life of the contract, it is important to set and adhere to realistic deadlines and to have safeguards in place to allow for proper regulation of the contract in the absence of an agreement.
- The provision of various utilities allowed cross-subsidization of less profitable areas and economies of scale.

4.

SELECTING PROJECTS

Turning a desirable concept into a realizable public-private partnership (PPP) project requires significant resources. Over the longer term, however, money spent on project preparation at the early stages is usually money well spent. While this principle is generally true of all public procurement, it is doubly true of PPPs, in which the public sector engages with and exposes the project to the scrutiny of third parties. After examining the stages of project selection, this chapter considers lessons derived from experience to date.

It is common practice to split the project selection phase into a series of steps (see figure 4.1), which are not taken in isolation, but rather in the context of government policies with specific objectives for the sector and a vision that embraces private participation as a way to achieve those objectives. Conducting a high-level review of the service need, analyzing the justification for a project, and assessing its initial prospects for delivery as a PPP—that is, making the "strategic business case"—are the first steps in project selection. Key advisers may be contracted at this stage to help the public sector with its decision making. Projects that are unlikely to deliver the government's overall policy requirements or that have few prospects as a PPP can be eliminated at an early stage, before incurring significant costs and damaging the credibility of the project and the government.

After initial analysis, the next step seeks to turn the projects with a greater chance of success into realistic opportunities for private sector participation through an initial market assessment, although projects may still be eliminated throughout the process. The selection and preparation of projects are rarely a tidy sequence of activities; instead the process is usually iterative, as one factor (such as affordability) affects another (such as project

Figure 4.1   Stages of Project Selection

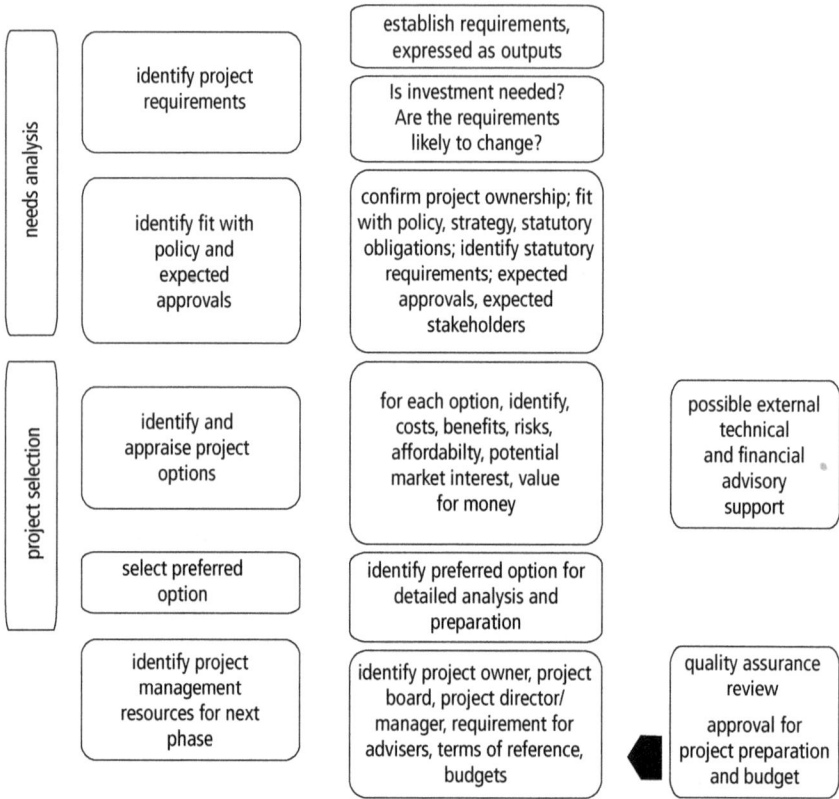

Source: Authors.

scope) and readjustments are made. Thus some of the key questions posed early on will be asked again at later stages; they may simply be addressed in less detail at the early strategic business case stage. Such issues need to be examined and retested throughout the process and will center around five main themes: the strategic justification for the project, whether the project represents value for money, whether the project is affordable, whether the project is commercially viable or bankable, and whether the authority has the right resources, skills, and organization to manage the process (United Kingdom, Her Majesty's Treasury n.d.). Broadly, these can be encapsulated in the following three questions:

- What are the project's scope and requirements and justification for these (the strategic case)?

- Can the project be delivered as a PPP (the affordability, commercial, and management cases)?
- Should the project be delivered as a PPP (the value for money case)?

Project Scope and Requirements

The basic rationale for a project may appear obvious—for example, to upgrade a major congested intercity road link or build a power-generating facility to meet rapidly increasing demand—and it may be part of an existing higher-level investment program, where the decision may already have been made at a policy level (hence the relevance of an investment plan).

But how many lanes should the road include, what should its alignment be, or would rail be a better option? One of the fundamental causes of project failure, for *both* traditional public sector procurement and PPPs, is often a lack of clarity on the part of the public authority regarding the exact scope and requirements of the project. At the outset, lack of clarity usually means change later on. If this happens during the procurement phase, then the level of private sector interest may be significantly reduced or the procurement phase will be drawn out, which can cause higher costs and delays for both parties and loss of competitive tension, itself a major driver of value for money. If change takes place during the construction or operating phases of a PPP, this may lead to significantly higher costs for the public sector. Clarity of scope should apply to all infrastructure projects. What distinguishes PPPs is that the long-term contractual relationship requires the public sector to be very clear from the start about the outputs needed from the project. The performance-based nature of the PPP also encourages the private sector party to focus on how it will deliver the output over the *long term* and to take into account the key interdependencies between design, construction, operation, maintenance, and performance.

A disciplined approach will involve establishing the detailed scope and requirements for the service need (this may be in relation to a more general policy already defined—for example, provision of health care to a sector of the community). This involves assessing the relative costs and benefits of different options for service delivery (for example, whether to refurbish or expand an existing hospital or build a new one). The detailed analysis of the option as to *how* the chosen service requirement may be procured is a subsequent exercise and is the subject of the section later in this chapter on "value for money." The extent of any analysis of different service delivery options (usually involving some form of cost-benefit analysis) will depend on the availability of reliable data and the ability to identify and measure the full costs and benefits of the project. It may also depend on the use of established tools such as an agreed public sector investment discount rate.

Expressing Projects in Terms of Outputs

Given the contractual nature of PPPs, particularly for availability-based PPPs, the public sector's requirements need to be expressed clearly in the form of an output requirement (for example, the availability and price of power or water or the quality of accommodation services in a school). If requirements or means of delivery are likely to change significantly over the contract period, locking into a long-term availability-based PPP may not be appropriate, as has been found with certain technology-rich projects. Other forms of partnering for such projects, however, can work well (see box 4.1), but these forms of PPP are outside the scope of this guide.

Traditional project procurement has usually focused on *inputs*, such as choice of building materials or a certain type of technology for a generation plant, and so PPPs may involve a fundamental change in the way projects are prepared and in the nature of the information that needs to be provided to private sector bidders. A collection of engineering studies, typically produced by a public works department used to viewing projects in terms of inputs, will not attract and engage the private sector in a PPP. Private sector investors expect to see in PPP contracts a clear set of *output requirements, associated standards,* and the *terms* by which they can expect to be paid for good performance. They want to understand from an early stage the risks they will be asked to assume.

For availability-based projects where the service delivery requirements need to be set out in considerable detail to determine the payments for making the public service available, this can be especially demanding. A useful rule when developing output requirements is that they should be SMART—specific, measurable, achievable, realistic, and timely—if they are eventually to form the basis of a contract (see table 4.1). The same principles can apply to a user-fee PPP (defining, for example, the service requirements in an airport concession or a rail service), which will be important for the regulator or other entity in charge of monitoring the contract and supervising compliance of the operator.

Can the Project Be Delivered as a Public-Private Partnership?

Once the scope and requirements of the project have been broadly identified, the next question to ask is whether it is feasible for the project to be delivered under a PPP structure. As mentioned, the steps of selecting and preparing projects are parts of an iterative process in which the scope and requirements are modified as the project requirements converge with what

BOX 4.1

Liverpool Direct

In 2001 the Liverpool City Council, faced with underinvestment in information technology infrastructure and with a badly integrated multitude of systems, entered into an 11-year strategic partnership with British Telecommunications worth £300 million.

The City Council was looking to change the quality of the services provided to citizens through the use of better information technology. Outdated technology, siloed information, and inefficient paper-based processes were among the problems it faced as one of the United Kingdom's (then) worst-performing local authorities. Apart from better systems and technology, a significant amount of change management with the attendant labor issues would also be involved. The City Council was determined to move away from the traditional models of client and contractor adversarial behavior and costly and bureaucratic contract monitoring arrangements. At the same time, it was looking for significant new investment combined with flexibility to meet the evolving needs of users. The services identified included call centers, customer contact centers, and payroll and human resource administration. A soft market-testing process was then used to confirm that such a package was likely to generate interest from suppliers with relevant experience.

The prequalification process focused on the experience, expertise, and financial capacity of bidders, and output specifications were developed for each part of the service. Four bidders were short listed.

The partnership involved a 20 percent equity share, and the involvement of the City Council through the Board in the service delivery vehicle. This enabled the City Council to be involved in strategic decisions and keep a close eye on delivery costs. Service levels and the timetables for enhanced service delivery were then agreed for each service component. The City Council is not liable for the losses of the joint venture.

The project has been successful, resulting in much higher levels of performance, even higher than those contractually committed to, with significant reductions in the costs of service delivery.

Table 4.1 An Example of Output Specifications for an Accommodation Public-Private Partnership

Characteristic	SMART	Not SMART
Specific	Refurbish or replace all dwellings on the estate to comply with the government's "decent homes" standard	Refurbish dwellings to a good standard
Measurable	Ensure that all dwellings are structurally sound, with adequate ventilation, lighting, and thermal comfort	Ensure that dwellings are fit for habitation
Achievable	Maintain internal temperature at X degrees when outside temperature is between Y and Z degrees	Ensure that internal temperature is always maintained at X degrees
Realistic	Ensure that faults with the temperature control system are rectified within eight hours during business hours and 16 hours outside business hours	Ensure that faults with the temperature control system are repaired within two hours
Timely	Maintain a log of faults and report every month	Provide an annual report on performance

Source: Authors.
Note: SMART = specific, measurable, achievable, realistic, and timely.

is possible for the private sector to deliver efficiently and cost-effectively and what is affordable. There are three key questions:

- Who will pay for the project and how (affordability)?
- What are the risks inherent in the project, and how should these be dealt with (risk allocation)?
- Will the resulting project be able to raise the required debt financing (bankability) and attract contractors and other equity investors?

The first two issues are dealt with in the following section. The issue of bankability is addressed in chapter 5, and the issue of management or governance of the process is dealt with in chapter 6. Specialist advisers usually play a major role in assisting the public authority in developing the answers to these questions (see chapter 7).

Affordability
Affordability—here understood in a broad sense—examines the level and structure of the project's overall revenue requirements in relation to the capacity of users, the public authority, or both to pay for the infrastructure

service. This requires building up a picture of the expected operating and maintenance costs of the project, together with the levels of cash flow required to repay the loans and provide a return to investors. To determine this, a financial model for the project is developed using the best estimates of capital, operating, and maintenance costs, appropriate cost escalation indexes, and assumed financing structure and terms; this model forecasts the cash flow over the proposed term of the PPP contract. Developing of the model is one of the main roles of the financial and technical advisers. At the early stages of project selection, this exercise may be conducted at a fairly general level, but it will involve increasing levels of detail during the project preparation stage. Assessing the private sector's capacity and willingness to deliver on the forecast basis forms an important part of the initial market assessment (discussed in more detail below).

In the case of user-fee PPPs, once the expected revenue requirements for the project have been established, the capacity and willingness of users to pay for the infrastructure service needs to be assessed. This may require significant changes to existing tariff levels. If a regulatory framework already exists in the sector, this will require harmonizing the requirements of the project with what is possible under the current regulatory regime; if this does not match the revenue requirements for the project, tariff adjustments may be needed, which could be difficult for regulators and policy makers. If no regulatory framework for the sector is yet in place, it may also require the establishment of a regulatory entity to implement the tariff policy set out in the concession agreement. The risks of such institutional reform being implemented simultaneously with a project bid may be unacceptable to private investors, or the private party may be prepared to assume such risks but will add to the costs of the project a charge for the risks, further affecting the tariff required. If the public sector will be required to make up the difference between what users are able or willing to pay and what the project needs in revenue over the operating period, will the private party accept the long-term government payment risk that is involved? This may lead to a requirement for larger government payments to meet part of the up-front capital costs (sometimes referred to as "viability gap funding"; see chapter 5), but are these affordable under the government budget constraints? Another associated question is whether the guarantee of such up-front government payments reduces the incentive of the contractor to perform.

For availability-based PPPs, where the public authority, not the user, makes the payments, assessment of affordability is one of the most important aspects in considering the deliverability of the project. These long-term payment obligations may present challenges for government (as well as investors), which in turn affect both the scope and level of services in the project design.

Options may need to be examined that combine direct fees from members of the public with government performance-based service payments or that contribute existing government assets to the project. Examples may include co-locating fee-paying and public medical facilities in the same hospital project or contributing publicly owned land that has high commercial potential in exchange for lower long-term service payments (Peterson 2009).

Project selection therefore involves an early assessment of what payment structure is feasible; what the government or the users can afford to pay (and when); what the impact will be on the project's scope, service level, and structure; and what associated risks the private sector might be prepared to accept. Although of less relevance for the private sector, this exercise helps the public sector to identify and manage any long-term fiscal obligations—implicit and explicit—that may result from PPPs. In the case study of the Mexican Bajío Regional Hospital, the private partner provides nonclinical services in return for a yearly payment from the government, while Mexico's Ministry of Health provides clinical services. Through the Projects for the Provision of Services (PPS) scheme, the government transfers the design, construction, equipment, operation, and administration risks to the service provider. The payment system is, therefore, directly associated with the continuing availability and quality of the physical assets and nonclinical services provided.

Risk Identification and Allocation
In addition to assessing the sources of revenue linked to affordability of the project, a complete picture of the risks that flow from the project requirements also needs to be established.

Risk Identification   Risk identification is a comprehensive exercise concerning matters and contingent events that are both internal and external to the project itself; it involves analyzing all phases of a project, notably project preparation, setting up of the project vehicle, funding, design, construction, commissioning, and operation, together with risks associated with legacy assets and services that may be transferred into the project following signature of the contract. Checklists of risks that typically apply to infrastructure projects can be used together with risk workshops in which the authority and relevant stakeholders can brainstorm the expected risks. A "risk register" can be used to record all risks and to serve as a checklist throughout the life of the project. This will usually list the nature of the risk, its probability of occurring, and its expected impact on the project, as well as the measures taken to mitigate those risks and how they have worked in practice (see the section on risk mitigation below). Advisers can play an important role in this process.

Risk Allocation   This involves allocating or sharing the responsibility for dealing with the consequences of each risk between the parties. The principle is to allocate the risk to the party best able to control its occurrence or manage its consequences as well as to the party in the best position to assess the likelihood of the risk arising within a context commercially acceptable to the private sector. There are only two parties to whom the risks can be allocated: the PPP contractor (that is, the private sector including its investors, lenders, subcontractors, insurers, and so forth) and the public body entering the PPP contract (ultimately, this risk rests with the users or taxpayers of the host country). Therefore, risks can be allocated to the private sector or to the public sector, but they also can be shared on an agreed basis by both sectors. The PPP contract will reflect the agreed allocation of risks and will include risk mitigation measures when deemed appropriate. Risk does not disappear through contractual structuring; it is simply reallocated among the parties.

Risks associated with design, technology, construction, and operation are typically allocated to the private sector, which is usually more efficient than government at controlling and managing them. This may vary between projects—for example, the tunneling section of a road construction project may be an unacceptable risk for the contractors, lenders, and investors due to the probability and the impact of the risk as a result of unknown geological conditions. Allocation of risks may also vary between markets depending on the appetite of the private parties and the level of competition. Other risks may be better managed by the public sector, such as regulatory, environmental, and foreign exchange risks, or may be shared, such as demand or change-of-law risks. In some countries certain risks will be allocated by law to the public or to the private sector for political or historical reasons, and any contractual arrangement to the contrary will have no legal effect. Therefore, legal constraints and the ability of the relevant party to assume a given risk must be taken into account regardless of which party is more efficient at controlling and managing the risks.

This exercise of risk allocation is one of the most important steps in assessing and developing the bankability of the project. This process also helps to identify the issues that the public authority should resolve at the project preparation stage. During this stage, a "risk matrix" can be employed, in conjunction with the "risk register," to record the proposed assignments of risk that will be reflected in the PPP contract (and measures adopted to mitigate those risks). Again, advisers can play an important role in this process. This will ensure that, if risks do in fact arise during the life of the project, both parties have agreed in the PPP contract what to do about them. Some risks may be allocated to specialist third parties such as insurers, and chapter 5 examines in more detail some of the instruments available to absorb project risks.

Risk Mitigation

It is important to reduce the likelihood of risks and their consequences for the risk taker. A change in project scope can sometimes reduce risk. For example, giving the private sector party control over the fuel transport facilities for a power generation project, and including this in the scope of the project, may reduce interface risks.

Risk Monitoring and Review

Risk management is an ongoing process that continues throughout the life of the project (see figure 4.2), and governments need to monitor all risks, even those allocated to third parties, because they are ultimately responsible for the adequate delivery of services to the public. Existing risks need to be monitored and new risks identified as the project develops and the environment changes. The contract management team will normally update the risk management plan, which is linked to the risk register, regularly throughout the life of the project.

Figure 4.2 Elements of a Risk Management Plan

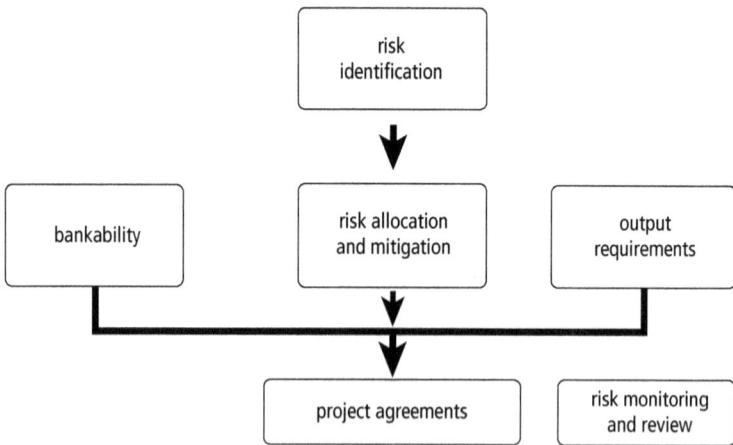

Source: Authors.

Should the Project Be Delivered as a Public-Private Partnership?

Even if a project can be delivered as a PPP, *should* it be? Comparing private and public alternatives to implement a given project is a sensible approach mainly for availability-based PPPs, where the flows of revenues—to be paid by the government—are known with sufficient certainty and there is a realistic alternative for a public sector project. In the case of user-fee PPPs, when the value of the PPP option will only be known after the bids have been submitted or where limitations on public sector funding preclude any publicly funded alternative, such comparison may appear not to be relevant. However, even for such projects, government still has to make important decisions about how its resources are deployed or the opportunity cost of giving up certain rights. For example, the grant of the concession for a user-fee toll road carries opportunity costs for government: the toll revenues, which are, after all, a form of tax, could otherwise be available to the public sector instead of to the private sector concessionaire, or any land rights in a highway concession could be exploited by the relevant public authority. In addition, "contingent liabilities" for the public authority (such as a guaranteed minimum level of use) are potential costs. These are important choices, and the risks or costs of delivering one form of project may significantly outweigh the perceived benefits. (Clearly, in assessing options and contingencies, their likelihood of materializing needs to be taken into account.)

Value for money (VfM) is one approach to identify and assess these choices. It is therefore a *relative* concept used to compare options. While the concept was developed largely in the United Kingdom in the early 1990s, it is also used in countries such as Australia, Canada, and the Netherlands for their project development programs. The use of the VfM is less prevalent in developing countries, although South Africa adopted this approach in 2000 to appraise PPP projects.[1] In the United Kingdom, VfM is defined as "the optimum combination of the whole of life cost and quality (or fitness for purpose) of the good or service to meet the user's requirements" (United Kingdom, Her Majesty's Treasury 2006). VfM looks at the costs and risks over the lifetime of the different project output delivery options and is linked in many ways to cost-benefit analysis, although this may depend on the nature of the sector: VfM in the social infrastructure sector can usually only mean long-run cost minimization with respect to a set of outputs or performance measures, taking into account the risks of delivery

---

[1] Discussing the VfM methodology is beyond the scope of this guide, but a great deal of information is publicly available on how various governments go about it (see, for example, Partnerships Victoria 2001, 2003b; South Africa, National Treasury 2004b; United Kingdom, Her Majesty's Treasury 2006).

and the certainty of payment for delivery—that is, for a specified standard of public service delivery or, if for different standards of public services (as between alternative delivery approaches or between bidders offering the same approach, then adjusting for these differences), the risk-adjusted long-term payment. The key point is that benefits are not monetized (as it is not always easy to do so) and so do not form part of the evaluation. Where methodologies for valuing (in monetary terms) education outcomes and health outcomes are used, the VfM analysis would then more closely resemble a cost-benefit analysis. In the case of economic infrastructure, it should generally be possible to value (that is, monetize) the benefits, and so the VfM analysis would also be a cost-benefit analysis. There can, however, be some confusion, since VfM is often taken to subsume cost-benefit analysis, although the strong point about VfM analysis is that it does focus on risk issues in a way that cost-benefit analysis does not always do.

While not necessarily directly relevant to the private sector's perception of the project, the value for money analysis can therefore, in principle, underpin the project rationale and the choice, or otherwise, of creating a PPP. It can also, in principle, underpin the allocation of risks (which is highly relevant to the private sector). This can reduce the chances that government will change its mind later on, which can damage the credibility of the entire PPP program in the eyes of investors.

Initially, highly quantitative approaches were developed by governments to assess value for money. These approaches usually looked at the risk-adjusted long-term costs of adopting the PPP option versus the costs of using traditional procurement (often referred to as the public sector comparator—or PSC), taking into account the higher costs of private capital and the associated transaction costs, but adjusting for the value of the risk transfer between the public and private sectors. This comparison of the PPP option with a PSC project, however, has been shown to have limitations in practice, because such quantitative analysis is only as good as the available data and other factors, such as the choice of discount rate and the challenges of monetizing some costs and benefits. There is always the danger of relying too heavily on quantitative analysis or, worse, using it to justify a decision that has already been made. It is now generally accepted in developed countries that a quantitative approach should be treated as only one aspect of project appraisal and that other qualitative assessments of the potential impact of choosing the PPP option, such as the expected degree of competition during the procurement phase, should also be taken into account.[2]

---

[2] When the VfM concept was introduced in the United Kingdom, there were some serious criticisms of the relevance, accuracy, and applicability of the PSC method for developing-country

Shifting the discussion of the VfM's measurement in the context of developing countries, especially in Africa, a recent publication by Leigland and Shugart (2006) reiterates the importance for governments to assess the rationale for using PPP options instead of traditional public sector methods to deliver infrastructure services. In that sense, using some type of comparison may help in documenting these choices and force the authorities to think carefully about the costs, the risks, and the best way of managing those risks. Developing an initial risk-adjusted financial model for a project may also be helpful for developing consensus among stakeholders about the desirable characteristics of the project. The authors suggest that a simplified version of such analysis could show the estimated transaction costs associated with alternative types of PPP and help to determine whether the likely efficiency gains would compensate for those costs. However, as has been found in more mature PPP markets, taking an overly complex and purely quantitative approach may not be the best tool for achieving those purposes. This can be the case especially in developing countries, since such analysis may be impossible to do properly, given the scarcity of data, the limited local expertise, and in some cases the lack of a viable public option. If these limitations are not recognized up-front, procuring authorities may risk wasting too many resources on an impossible task or, worse, wasting them to justify a foretold decision. Nevertheless, output-based and payment-for-performance contracts are at the heart of VfM in PPP. The justification for adopting a PPP scheme therefore needs to take this into account, whether through a PSC or otherwise.

Finally, governments may decide to go ahead with a PPP project for reasons beyond only the financial consideration. They may also consider the case for a PPP project in light of its potential impact beyond the project itself, its capacity to be replicated, and its wider policy benefits. An example is the principle of contestability. Providing a public service through a PPP can drive improvement through providing an alternative competing approach driving wider change or reform, in effect holding up a mirror to the existing methods of delivering public services.

Initial Market Assessment

At this stage of the project selection process, a reasonably well-developed picture of the project's scope and its output, construction, operating, and

---

governments (as discussed in Leigland and Shugart 2006). The U.K. Treasury (United Kingdom, Her Majesty's Treasury 2004, 2006) further developed guidance on value for money assessment, recommending, among others, using the PSC in conjunction with other more qualitative tests and reshaping the PSC into part of an early rigorous economic appraisal of an individual project.

funding requirements should be available. Projects that are unlikely to be affordable, or whose funding requirements are clearly outside the scope of what may be available, can be eliminated quickly. For other projects, the answer may not be so clear. Provided that the public authority can provide a reasonably coherent picture of the intended scope and requirements of the project, it is well placed to initiate a constructive dialogue with the private sector—investors, lenders, and contractors—on the feasibility of the project's scope and to establish the potential number of suppliers in the market. Such market sounding is discussed in detail in chapter 8.

Lessons from Experience: How the Private Sector Has Addressed Key Risks in Projects

An examination of recent PPP projects from around the world provides some useful starting points from which to understand which sectors and types of PPP projects appear to have been developed more successfully than others. This can be analyzed by looking at some of the key risks involved, whether or not the private sector was prepared to address them, and how they managed them. Broadly, the most common causes for project failure tend to involve one or a combination of revenue or market forecasts being wrong, failure of technology, insolvency of subcontractors, or excessive exchange rate fluctuations.

Tariff Reform Risk

Even in the more traditional publicly provided infrastructure sectors, users have many times been subsidized by governments (often at the expense of maintenance of the infrastructure asset itself), and so a realistic assessment of the true costs of subsidy may reveal that either a higher level of government support or significant tariff reform is needed. Both of these issues can carry significant risk for the private sector.

Sectors such as water or passenger rail, where revenue growth is often affected by challenges related to the level or collection of fees, are likely to be particularly difficult because of traditional underpricing and the political capital associated with these sectors. Here, private sector involvement may often be limited to management contracts or operating leases not involving significant capital investment. Government support will need to continue in parallel to fill the revenue gap until tariffs allow cost recovery. In contrast, mobile telephony, which does not have a legacy of below-cost pricing or the social and political sensitivities of water, has been one of the largest recipients of private sector investment.

Demand Risk and Capital Investment

Investors look closely at how the risk that they might bear of fluctuations in the use of the service (demand risk) is rewarded by the financial returns available and the timing and level of investment to which they are committed. For projects with high growth prospects, such as mobile telephony, investors generally consider such risk to be acceptable, especially as investment can be made in stages to fund incremental expansion of capacity and to take advantage of the potential commercial benefits of related services such as mobile banking. Where heavy initial investment is required, and the level of demand and prospects for growth are less certain, investors may be more circumspect. The different risk profile is reflected in the type of PPP transaction chosen. This is illustrated by figure 4.3, with concession projects involving rehabilitation of existing infrastructure and where use is already established, dominating in the transport sector. Overestimation of user demand is one of the principal causes of project failure in this sector. Of course, in most availability-based PPPs (not reflected in the data), demand risk usually resides with the public sector. However, this may present other constraints, such as the long-term creditworthiness of the government as purchaser of the service. In sectors such as urban rail transport, projects where demand risk is shared are often more stable than those that rely wholly on user demand.

Figure 4.3 Number of Projects with Private Participation in Infrastructure, by Sector and Type of Contract, 1996–2008

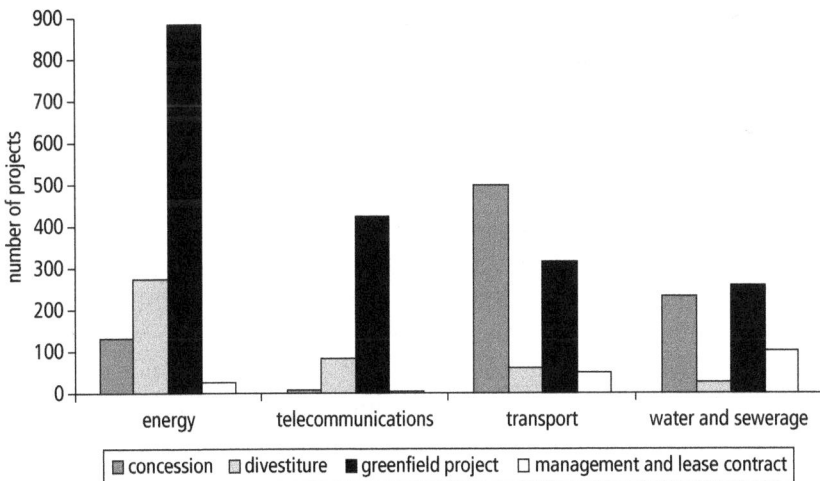

Source: World Bank and PPIAF PPI project database.

In this case, the project revenues could comprise a mix of both (reduced) passenger revenue and a performance-based availability fee from government. The public sector "subsidy" could otherwise be provided in the form of a partial payment of the capital costs. However, this mechanism, while it reduces the amount of private finance required and may be easier to administer, misses out on the important opportunity for government to link any subsidy to long-term performance. It can also expose the project to a more variable demand-dependent revenue stream.

Rehabilitation Risk

Investors have concerns about taking on the rehabilitation of existing assets, particularly in the energy and, to an extent, the water sectors or infrastructure assets like tunnels. This is reflected in the smaller share of concession contracts shown in figure 4.3, although for the reasons set out above, this may be less of an issue for some transport projects. These concerns relate to assets where the condition may be hard to assess (for example, a power generation plant or an underground water delivery network; see Leigland and Butterfield 2006). Other complications may arise out of the need to transfer an existing workforce or amend off-take contractual arrangements that are already in place. Sometimes, a management contract will be used initially to enable the private party to learn more about the underlying assets before moving to a more capital-intensive PPP.

Environmental and Other Physical Risks

Large infrastructure projects can also present environmental risks that may make investors wary, especially for greenfield projects. Transport and power projects may have adverse environmental and social impacts requiring project revaluation, redesign, additional investment, compensation costs, and strong stakeholder engagement, as well as reputational risks for participants. Thus, despite significant hydropower potential in many emerging markets, the number of such projects funded by the private sector has so far been small in comparison with other forms of power generation. Long lead times are often needed to address environmental issues. There may be significant geotechnical uncertainties and long construction periods; this can make project financing difficult and expensive for hydroelectric plants (unless they are run-of-the-river plants and do not require an investment in costly dams) due to the long gap between investment and revenue generation.

Interface Risk

For projects whose output, such as power generation, is purchased by another utility, investors pay close attention to the terms of any agreement to provide and purchase the project inputs or outputs and the reliability and creditworthiness of the interfacing party (often a state-owned entity). If the connecting infrastructure is not in place or needs to be rehabilitated, investors will want to know how this will be addressed, which, in turn, raises questions about who is responsible, where the funding will come from, whether the required infrastructure will be available when it is needed by the project, and what conditions will attach in the event that it is not. This can make such projects highly complex, as investors will need to analyze all the risks, not just those of the immediate project but also those of other projects on which it is dependent for supply or sales (that is, the *external* interface risks; see box 4.2). The São Paulo Metro Line 4 project is an

---

BOX 4.2

Regional Projects

Infrastructure projects can be regional in nature. This characteristic can present added complexity, involving different jurisdictions and multiple procurement and regulatory authorities.[1] This can place further pressure on governments (and create additional risks), as the private sector does not expect to have to resolve jurisdictional issues. If it finds itself having to resolve such issues, the private sector will begin to question the level of public sector commitment to the project. Thus, throughout the project preparation and tendering process, additional attention will need to be paid to the following:

- Clear ownership of the project, especially at the country level
- Alignment of policies among the relevant governments as they affect the project
- Clear, appropriately aligned legal and procurement processes
- Appropriate joint governance and approval processes, with the delegation of suitable authorities from the respective governments
- Design and operation of the public sector party responsible for drawing up and managing the contracts
- Existence and role of regional regulation in the oversight of contracts
- Possible need for common technical, safety, environmental, social, and other operating standards.

Note: 1. For a discussion of the role of regulation in a regional context and a review of several projects that cover more than one country or jurisdiction, see Woolf (2009).

example of how this issue has been addressed through the contractual structure (see the case study in chapter 5). The private sector is, however, often
better than government at managing the risks of integrating different components of a project.

Funding and Foreign Currency Risk

Projects without revenues linked to foreign currency are likely to face the
most significant constraints in many countries, due to the limited availability of long-term local-currency finance. In Sub-Saharan Africa, where
local-currency long-term funding is not available in many states, seaport
projects, which generally enjoy foreign currency–denominated revenue,
have been more numerous than road projects, which usually earn revenues
in local currency (see figure 4.4).

As local capital markets develop, however—evidenced by the issuance of
local-currency financial instruments with terms of up to 15–20 years, coupled with the use of risk mitigation instruments and strong domestic development finance institutions—long-term sources of local-currency funding may
increasingly be the principal source of funding for well-structured projects.

Other Considerations When Selecting PPP Projects

In addition to the revenue, demand, rehabilitation, environmental, interface,
funding, currency, and other risks mentioned above, there are other issues to

Figure 4.4 Number of Transport Projects in Sub-Saharan Africa in the World Bank PPI Database, by Sector, 1996–2007

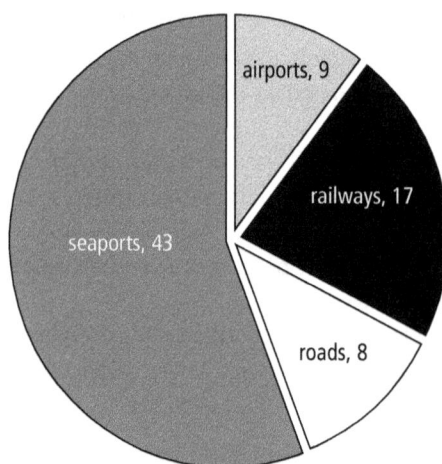

Source: World Bank and PPIAF PPI project database.

consider when assessing risk allocation and potential private sector interest in a PPP project:

- *Size.* Projects that are too small may have difficulty attracting corporate private sector interest, as the costs of preparing and managing the project will be high in relation to the investment required (and from the public sector's perspective, the transaction costs may be too high in relation to the size of the project). Conversely, projects that are too large may exceed the capacity of bidders and sources of finance (and, from the public sector's perspective, may make it difficult to transfer risks effectively not only at the procurement stage but also in the event that things go wrong later and a replacement party is required).
- *Geography and complexity.* Projects may be the right size for the market, but if they involve numerous smaller components that are geographically dispersed or remote, investors may be wary of the delivery and management costs and risks involved. Bundling smaller projects to make larger ones may not always be feasible.
- *Technology.* Lenders are particularly wary of using unproven technology or using proven technology in novel circumstances; the solid waste treatment sector is a good example of this issue.
- *Workforce.* Investors are concerned about how the public sector manages workforce issues, particularly in projects that may transfer significant staff from the public sector.
- *Subcontractor solvency.* If a subcontractor responsible for a key part of the project gets into financial difficulty, the project as a whole can be seriously affected. Lenders will look closely at the financial health of the various subcontractors, and this may sometimes make the participation of smaller contractors without a financial track record more challenging.

Case Study: Hospital Regional de Alta Especialidad del Bajío, Guanajuato State, Mexico

Project:	Hospital Regional de Alta Especialidad del Bajío y Unidad de Apoyo
Description:	25-year contract to design, build, finance, equip, operate, and maintain a 184-bed regional hospital and specialized medical support unit in the state of Guanajuato, Mexico
Financial close:	December 2005
Capital value:	US$230 million (78 percent is debt and 22 percent is equity)
Consortium:	Acciona
Financiers:	BVA

Mexico's rapid economic and demographic growth over the last decade has put pressure on the country's health care system. Despite of the government's efforts to provide increased health care services to its growing population, Mexico's hospital infrastructure suffers from years of underinvestment, and the country's hospital network is not dense enough to reach the entire population.

To address these problems, in 2002 the Mexican government launched an ambitious health care infrastructure program (Plan Nacional de Desarrollo y Programa Sectorial de Salud). This coincided with the development of its PPP program, which was called Projects for the Provision of Services (PPS).

The government first created a central PPP unit in the federal Ministry of Finance (Hacienda) to get Mexico's PPS scheme off the ground. Accessing overseas experience from other PPP units, the government developed a PPP policy tailored to Mexico's administrative, legal, and market environment. The government took advice in selecting the initial pilot projects based on their suitability for the PPS approach and high probability of success as well as in developing the PPS policy, which included approaches to the selection and management of professional advisers, the strategy for approaching the markets, and the assessment of value for money. Other challenges included ensuring that such projects would be well supported both by their respective line ministries and by the contractor and financing markets. The PPS team in the Ministry of Finance worked closely with the project delivery team in the Ministry of Health and identified the Hospital Regional de Alta Especialidad del Bajío (HRAEB) as a pilot project that could potentially be procured as a PPS project.

After three years of policy, program, and project preparation, the tender for the HRAEB was launched in March 2005. (At the same time three pilot projects in the transport and education sectors were also successfully launched.) A series of formal consultation processes took place before the formal launch of the bidding process, which, together with advisory input, helped to ensure the development of a bankable contract. After a well-orchestrated competitive process, Mexico's Ministry of Health granted the Spanish group Acciona a 25-year contract to design, build, finance, equip, operate, and maintain the 184-bed regional hospital with long-term finance from private sector banks. After 11 months of construction and three months of pre-operation, the HRAEB opened in April 2007.

The private partner provides nonclinical services in exchange for a yearly payment from the government, while Mexico's Ministry of Health provides clinical services. Through the PPS scheme, the government has transferred the design, construction, equipment, operation, and administration risks to the service provider. The payment system is, therefore, directly associated with the continuing availability and quality of the physical assets and accommodation services provided.

HRAEB was the first PPP hospital in Latin America and the first of a program of eight specialized hospitals in Mexico, which also include Ciudad Victoria (now completed), Ixtapaluca (now awarded), Acapulco, Chihuahua, Culiacán, Querétaro, and Torreón.

The following key lessons were derived from the project:

- Spending time and effort on developing the PPP policy frameworks and institutions up-front, followed by diligent individual project selection and preparation, is important.
- Careful branding of a PPP program constitutes an important communication tool.
- Taking a program, as opposed to a one-off project, approach helps to achieve efficiency and effectiveness overall.
- Selecting early projects based on their strong likelihood of success as PPPs helps to kick-start PPP programs.
- Establishing a PPP unit in a cross-sectoral ministry such as the Ministry of Finance helps to support the development of programwide approaches as well as the line ministry project delivery teams.

- While policy and program leadership is the government's responsibility, experienced and well-managed advisers can speed up and add value to program and project planning, procurement, and management activities.
- The importance of finance and sector ministries that work well together and the support of the sector ministry for the project cannot be overstated. It is also important to ensure that demand for the asset is well established, although this is more an issue of project selection than PPP procurement.
- PPP principles can be applied to delivering social infrastructure projects in emerging countries, provided that the specificities of each sector are understood, effort has gone into understanding the interest and concerns of the private contractors and funders, the procuring authority's requirements are well understood, and the contract and compensation systems are established in advance.

5.

FINANCING PPP PROJECTS

The financing of public-private partnership (PPP) projects is a large subject. This chapter provides a general introduction to the topic.[1]

Private sector finance for PPP projects normally consists of a mixture of equity, provided by investors in the project, and third-party debt, provided by banks or through financial instruments such as bonds. The equity investment is "first in, last out"—that is, in principle any losses that the project suffers are borne first by the investors, and lenders begin to suffer only if the equity investment is lost. It follows from this that equity investment has a higher risk than debt, and so equity investors expect a higher return for this risk. Since equity is therefore more expensive than debt, the more debt a project can raise, the lower its overall funding costs will be.

The technique generally used to raise a high proportion of debt for PPP projects is known as "project finance." This can provide as much as 70–90 percent of the total funding requirement—the ratio of debt to equity (known as gearing or leverage) depends on the perceived risks of the project. Project finance is sometimes referred to as limited-recourse finance, because the lenders' security is normally limited solely to the project, comprising, primarily, the project's cash flows and the sponsor's equity that is invested in a company set up especially for the project. This company is ring fenced from the rest of the project sponsor's business and prohibited from entering into any business outside the project. There is therefore a clear management focus on, and full transparency of, cash flows over the life of the

---

[1] For a more comprehensive introduction to PPP financing, see Delmon (2009, forthcoming 2011); Yescombe (2002, 2007).

project. The sponsors do not guarantee the project as a whole, and the lenders therefore rely on the cash flow of the project alone to repay the loan and pay interest (together known as debt service).[2] This is quite different from corporate finance—the more usual basis on which banks lend to businesses—where lenders generally rely on the strength of a company's balance sheet and covenants linked to overall performance of a diversified business as the source of cash flow and security for their loan rather than the singular performance of an individual asset or investment. In general, a PPP project's physical assets have little value if they are not used in the project, and private sector lenders cannot be allowed, for public policy reasons, to take security over them. (For example, a bank would not be allowed to foreclose on a road or a hospital and sell it off to the highest bidder.) Therefore, the main assets that lenders can rely on as security are the *contract* between the public authority and the private sector project entity and the *cash flows* deriving from this contract.

Projects can be financed using corporate finance—that is, lenders lend to the construction and operating and maintenance contractors, which in turn fund the project. This may create more flexible structures—at a price. But if the costs or complexity of project finance are prohibitive because of limited capacity, then this may be the preferred approach. However, contractors often only have limited capacity to take on debt, especially if the project is large in relation to their business. They may prefer to limit their risks through an equity investment in a stand-alone project, for example, if they are lending to a new overseas market and wish to minimize their exposure to host-country risks. Project finance is therefore often a more *efficient* way for lenders and investors to finance major infrastructure investments by the private sector as well as increase the availability of financing. It is normal for the public authority to let the bidders decide whether or not to use project finance and allow the competitive process to drive the most efficient funding structure. However, it is important for the public authority to understand clearly the overall capacity and capability of the lending markets when implementing a PPP program, and there may be steps it can take to encourage the development of such markets.

Lenders and Risk: Bankability

The identification and allocation of risk between the public authority and the investors are discussed in chapter 4. However, the issue of risk is not just a matter for discussion between the public authority and private sector bidders for a PPP project: the lenders play a major role in this respect.

---

[2] In certain cases, the assets underlying the project may also provide security for lenders.

Banks earn a relatively low return (after allowing for their own funding costs) compared to equity investors, but the corollary to this is that they cannot afford to take high risks, the realization of which could easily wipe out the return they had expected to make. Therefore, when considering risk allocation, the public authority must bear in mind that allocating a high level of risk to the private sector will reduce the amount that lenders are willing to lend to the project, and so increase its cost, since the gap will have to be filled up with more—higher-priced—equity. The correct allocation and mitigation of risk are major factors in making projects bankable, and the public authority needs to develop a clear understanding of how potential lenders perceive the risks of the project from the early stages of project selection and preparation. This is one of the matters requiring the assistance of a financial adviser.

Since the project company will often be a special-purpose company with limited assets of its own, project lenders take a strong interest in the long-term performance of the project on which the repayment of their loans depends. They also play a useful role in reviewing the financial viability of the project on which their decision to lend will be based (a process known as due diligence) and in helping to ensure that the infrastructure asset is constructed on time and on budget, is properly maintained, and operates within budget.

Lenders also want to ensure that the risks allocated to the project company, to which they are lending, are passed on as much as possible and in the most efficient way, to the various subcontractors who will build and operate the project. The lenders have a strong interest in the financial strength and technical capability of the subcontractors, in addition to the terms of the PPP contract between the public authority and the project entity. The availability of banks willing and able to provide project financing is therefore linked to the availability of strong and capable contractors prepared and able to operate in the market concerned (which is one of the reasons why "market sounding," discussed in chapter 8, is so important). Box 5.1 summarizes the major concerns of project lenders.

Having loans at risk to the performance of the project drives many of the benefits of the PPP process: since the lenders have a long-term risk exposure to the PPP project, they should take a long-term view of its viability and continue to monitor performance closely.

In many emerging markets, the domestic banking sector may have neither the capacity nor the experience to provide all of the long-term debt required for PPP projects. Similarly, the international banking market may have concerns about long-term risk exposures in the country concerned. Moreover, international lenders may not be able to provide finance in the currency of

Major Concerns of Project Lenders

- Certainty of the project cash flows for meeting debt service requirements
- Bankability of public sector obligations
- Soundness and stability of the legal framework for PPP
- Effectiveness and enforceability of the PPP contract and related agreements
- Confidence in the regulatory regime when applicable
- Right to step in if a project fails and availability of alternative contractors
- Ability of contractors to perform and the quality of their management
- Bankability of contractors and quality of contractor guarantees
- Risks that are understood, controllable, finite, and appropriately allocated
- Reputation impact of the project (environmental, social)
- Availability and effectiveness of insurance cover, where needed.

See also the list of bankability concerns for overseas lenders in the following section.

the project's home country. But if the project's cash flow does not match the proposed currency of its debt, there is clearly a substantial exchange rate risk, which lenders would not normally find acceptable. In some emerging markets, especially in Asia and Latin America, the problem may be less acute due to the existence of strong domestic lending markets in some countries and, potentially, even the availability of long-term capital market finance from institutions such as pension funds. Third-party public equity may also be available through the public markets, especially for projects that are operational or seeking to expand. Thus the financing challenges will vary considerably between countries.

One of the early considerations in assessing the bankability of a project is the availability of long-term funding that matches the currency of the project revenue. The tenor of the debt also has an impact on the affordability of the project: longer-term debt implies lower annual capital repayments and therefore lower annual costs.

Fixed interest rates will help to reduce changes in these costs. Projects financed by long-term fixed-price debt are inherently less flexible than shorter-term projects or projects financed on the basis of a variable-interest (floating) rate as lenders will protect themselves against the costs of early termination of their finance, which fixed-price debt usually involves. So there is a trade-off between affordability and flexibility. Flexibility costs money.

Contract Terms: Bankability

The lenders therefore pay very close attention to the terms of the PPP concession or project agreement, as this sets out how the various project risks will be allocated between the public and private sector parties. Set out below are some of the key areas of a project that will receive the closest attention from lenders (in addition to those highlighted in box 5.1):

- Protection of lender rights (for example, security rights, priority in insolvency)
- Political risk
- Force majeure
- Expropriation
- Early-termination payments
- Residual value of project assets upon termination
- Dispute resolution and enforcement.

In addition to the contractual negotiations that may take place around these provisions, various risk mitigation instruments, discussed below, may be available for tackling these issues.

Equity Investment

Apart from debt, the balance of funding consists of equity, usually made available by the main construction or operation and maintenance contractors or by third-party financial investors. These potential equity investors usually lead the bid for the project. Equity funding is needed because the lenders require some cushion between the cash flow available from the project after it has met the operating and maintenance costs and the cash flow required to service their debt. Equity therefore plays a vital role in absorbing project risk and facilitating debt funding. Third-party equity investors (that is, those with no other contractual relationship with the project) can also be useful in sorting out any problems that may arise between the other private sector parties, as the return on their investment depends on the performance of the project contractors. See box 5.2 for the major concerns of contractors and investors.

Contractual Relationships

A PPP structure involves not just the contractual relationship between the public and private sectors, but also the web of contracts governing the relationship between the private sector parties themselves and the allocation of

Major Concerns of Contractors and Investors

- Cost, time, and quality of the PPP bid process: Are major approvals (such as for land) still pending?
- Clarity and stability of the legal and regulatory framework
- Criteria for evaluating bids
- Quality of the public sector project team and its advisers
- Security of the project's income stream (demand, bankability of public sector obligations)
- Deliverables and assessment of performance: What are they expected to deliver, and how will their performance be measured?
- Availability and cost of long-term debt funding
- For financial investors, track record of the construction contractor and operator to deliver the service on time and on budget
- Status and availability of connecting infrastructure and availability of inputs and terms of supply
- Effectiveness and enforceability of the PPP contract and related agreements
- Potential foreign exchange risks
- Wider operating environment for private capital
- Allocation of risks both between the public and private sectors and among the private parties
- Returns commensurate with the risks they are asked to assume
- Effectiveness with which the public sector will manage the contract and make decisions
- Opportunities to refinance the debt or sell the investment.

risks among them: in addition to the different lenders and equity investors involved, the entities building the asset and those operating it are often different. This is summarized in figure 5.1. The special-purpose project company is the vehicle that brings all of these contractual relationships together within the private sector. This has important implications for the bidding process: private sector bidders need to be given enough time—and they need to have confidence in the seriousness of the public authority's intentions— to spend the not inconsiderable resources assembling the components for a high-quality bid. It is the special-purpose project company that should take

Figure 5.1 Typical Contractual Structure of a Public-Private Partnership

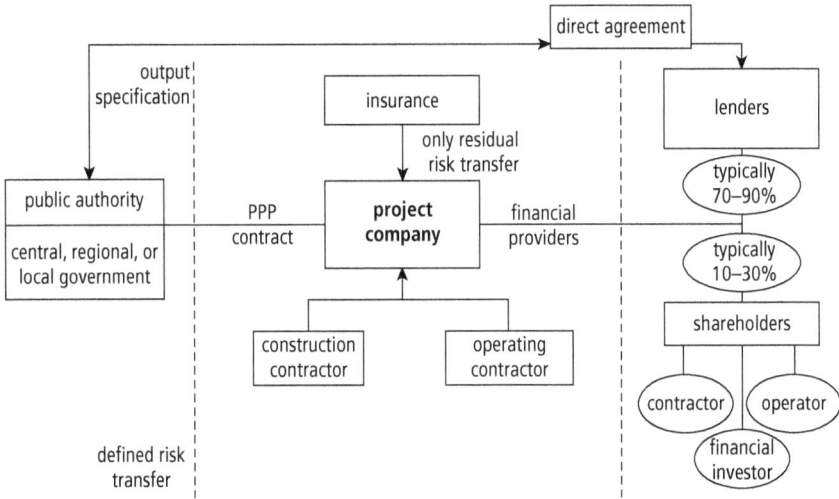

Source: Authors.

and manage the integration risk of these different subcontactors, providing a single, seamless service for the public authority. If a project fails, the public authority will look to the special-purpose project company, and it is up to the project company to allocate the risk among its subcontractors (or bear the risk itself). The lenders want to be sure that the matrix of subcontracts fits together and that the special-purpose project company is adequately staffed and resourced to manage them.

As shown in figure 5.1, there may also be a direct contractual relationship between the public authority and the lenders. This is not a guarantee, but a mechanism to govern the project if the contractors do not perform as promised and the lenders need to "step into" the shoes of the special-purpose project company and assume certain rights and responsibilities while alternative contractor arrangements are sorted out. They are, in effect, doing what the public authority might otherwise have to do in sorting out problems in conventionally procured projects. Thus step-in rights are a help to the public authority as well as an essential part of the project's bankability, helping to align the lenders' interests with those of the authority.

Refinancing

In many markets the availability of committed long-term funding over the life of the project, say, 25 years, may not be possible; indeed, even in mature PPP markets it can be a challenge as the events of the credit crisis have shown. Lenders who may only be prepared to lend for five to seven years may still be willing to lend to the project, but on the basis that a new lender will replace their debt at that later point (these are often referred to as "mini-perm" structures). The issue arising is: Who bears the risk in the event that replacement financing cannot be found when the current debt matures (or even if it can, the underlying interest rates may have gone up so much that the project's cash flow is no longer sufficient to cover debt service)? In markets where there is confidence that replacement debt will be available in the future, the risk is usually borne by the equity investors. The risk is that if a replacement lender cannot be found, then all project revenues—after operating costs—go to pay off the loans (so that no return on equity accrues) until a replacement is found or, at worst, the lenders declare a project default. In less liquid markets, equity investors may not be prepared to accept such risks, hence the need for partial credit guarantees or longer-maturity forms of public finance, which are discussed later in this chapter.

The issue of refinancing may also arise in another way. Once an infrastructure asset is built and operating satisfactorily, many of the initial project risks will fade away. Similarly, the lending environment for PPPs may improve over time, in part due to development of the program by the public sector. Thus the perceived risks of the program and hence the component projects may fall. This may open the opportunity to replace the existing debt finance with new lending on more competitive terms (lower lending margin, longer tenor, or even higher amounts of debt in relation to equity). Equity investors have a strong incentive to take advantage of these improved terms, as this can lead to the opportunity to extract cash from the project more quickly, leading to a substantial increase in their returns without necessarily affecting the underlying terms of the deal with the public authority. One of the reasons this form of refinancing is so contentious is that it breaches the "first in, last out principle" of equity referred to at the start of the chapter, so governments must have a policy on this form of refinancing. Mechanisms often exist to ensure that any benefits that may arise from refinancing the existing debt on better terms are shared between the equity investors (who, after all, have taken substantial project risks) and the public authority (who, it would argue, has been responsible for the improved environment). It can also be politically challenging for the private sector to be seen to benefit excessively and exclusively from such gains. The basis upon which such gains are shared needs to be agreed in the PPP contract, along with effective mechanisms to deal with it. This may be particularly relevant for new markets or for markets where current terms of debt finance may be expected to improve over time.

Risk Mitigation and Other Sources of Project Funding

Mobilizing private sector funding, especially long-term funding, is one of the key challenges for PPP projects, especially in emerging markets. The challenge is especially significant during periods of dislocation of international credit markets, such as during 2008–09. This may be due to issues of liquidity (that is, constraints on the *supply side* for long-term finance, reflecting either finance capacity issues or perceptions of risk that are *external* to the project itself, such as general political or market risks), to the perceived risks of the project *itself*, or to a combination of these factors. It is important to distinguish between these different issues, as they may require different solutions. The global financial crisis of 2008–09, for example, reflected general financial sector market, capital, and liquidity risks, while the underlying risks of many PPP projects may not have changed significantly (although the income effects of the crisis may lead to a slowdown in the demand for some services).

Since raising long-term debt and equity capital remains a challenge in many developing countries, various mechanisms have been and continue to be developed, particularly by development finance institutions (DFIs) and governments around the world, to mitigate the risks—either general or project specific—that might otherwise prevent lenders and investors from funding projects. The São Paulo Metro Line 4 project (see the case study at the end of this chapter) is a good example of how DFIs can help to achieve financial close on large complex PPPs in difficult and often unanticipated market conditions. Public sector financing for the construction of the metro tunnels was provided by the World Bank and the Japan Bank for International Cooperation, while financing for the concessionaire was led by the Inter-American Development Bank (IDB). Essentially the various approaches seek either to transfer certain defined risks to third parties that have an acceptable credit or investment standing or to fill the gaps left by what the private sector is not prepared to fund. Bilateral or multilateral institutions that have strong international credit ratings are often prepared to take on such risks, as they have the capacity to assess, absorb, and manage them. In this way, they can also use their resources to encourage or develop further approaches to private sector financing. The issue is to identify what specific risks are preventing private sector lenders and investors from supporting the project and then see if methods of mitigating these risks are available. This is often one of the roles of the financial adviser.

Types of Risk Mitigation

Risk mitigation instruments usually vary depending on whether they seek to cover *all* of the loss or a *part* of the loss that could be suffered by the lender or investor; they may only support *debt funding,* by covering credit risk issues, or they may support *equity funding,* by covering investment risk issues (for fuller details on risk mitigation, see Matsukawa and Habeck 2007). They may also depend on whether the risks relate to *political risks* and other forms of nonproject-specific risks or to *commercial* or *project risks.* There can be combinations of these risks: credit guarantees may cover all or part of the debt service of a loan instrument regardless of whether the cause for default is political or commercial. While this complicates efforts to categorize the various approaches to risk mitigation, the following sections look at this issue in two broad categories: forms of *guarantee* and forms of *funding.*

Partial-Credit Guarantees

Partial-credit guarantees are often used to enhance the borrower's access to long-term credit markets by seeking to share the credit risk between lenders and the provider of the guarantee. DFIs may issue these guarantees, which in particular may be used to cover the "tail-end" repayments due on a long-term project-finance loan. This encourages private sector banks to lend to the PPP project, even though they do not want their loan to be outstanding for the full life of the project.

Full-Credit or "Wrap" Guarantees

The most comprehensive forms of credit risk cover may involve the entire project debt being guaranteed by another entity, which effectively steps into the shoes of the lender by assuming the project risk that the lender might otherwise take. In this case, the lender is interested mainly in the credit risk of such a guarantor and no longer in that of the project itself. Hitherto, providers of such guarantees have been large private insurance companies known as monoline insurers. However, following the disruption of the international financial market during 2008–09, the monoline insurers had less capacity to participate in the project finance market. Providers of credit guarantees can facilitate long-term funding from sources that may not traditionally take project risk—typically pension funds. In this case, the lending instrument is usually a bond that investors can hold or sell to each other, rather than a bank loan provided directly to the project. The underlying provision of long-term debt funding is essentially the same. However, even before the recent downturn in international financial markets, this form of guarantee had rarely been used in emerging economies, with only a few examples, such as the roads sector in Chile.

Export Credit Agencies

A more common form of credit risk cover in emerging economies is provided by export credit agencies. Originally established to cover political risks only, export credit agencies increasingly provide cover for both political and commercial risks. These are usually government entities, which are keen to promote their country's exports by providing such risk cover for long-term loans used to finance the purchase of their exports. As a consequence, the provision of such cover is usually, but not always, "tied" to the value and nationality of the goods exported for the project or the lender involved. Depending on the country, such cover may be for up to 100 percent of the political and commercial risk associated with the underlying cost being financed. Apart from the risk cover, these entities may also provide advantages in the form of long-term competitive interest rates.

Debt Underpinning

Another approach to mobilizing long-term private sector debt funding is sometimes achieved by the public authority itself guaranteeing repayment of a portion of the project debt even if the cause of the potential default lies with the private sector partner—this is known as "debt underpinning." Clearly this approach only works if the long-term creditworthiness of the public authority is acceptable to the lenders. This approach should usually be seen as part of a program to stimulate the development of long-term sources of private sector funding (it may also reduce the overall cost of funding to the project), while at the same time the portion that is guaranteed is unlikely to be affected if the project gets into difficulty. In this approach, as the procuring authority itself is guaranteeing a part of the debt, it is important that the *unguaranteed* portion of the debt is sufficient to ensure that the lenders will have enough of their own funds at risk to be concerned with to the performance of the project. This is important to ensure that they carry out proper due diligence and management of project performance, a fundamental principle of PPPs. This requires balancing the realities of the market and the strategic aim to encourage market development with the potential disincentives that underpinning debt in this way may create for effective risk transfer. Clearly, as with any government guarantee mechanism, there may also be significant fiscal implications as a result of the contingent liabilities that result from this approach.

Political Risk Guarantees and Guarantee Funds

Political risk guarantees or insurance protect lenders and investors against losses due to defined political events, such as currency nonconvertibility or transfer risks, expropriation, or war, as opposed to the commercial risks of the project itself. Providers of such political risk cover can be multilateral or bilateral institutions or private insurance companies. More recently, risks associated with the actions or inactions of government or a breach of contract (usually after arbitration award) have been covered by such instruments.

This can be particularly relevant for PPPs that rely on the long-term effectiveness of concession agreements and the long-term nature of government obligations that may lie behind them.

Given the importance of a well-functioning regulator, especially for many user-fee PPPs, a related form of guarantee can be used to protect against defined regulatory risks. This form of insurance pays the investor an amount of money if the investor can demonstrate that the regulator or government failed to comply with the preestablished regulatory framework, especially with regard to tariff setting. As the guarantee is normally provided by an entity such as the World Bank that the government must reimburse in the event of a payment being made, such form of guarantee can act as a strong incentive to ensure fair operation by the regulator. It is important, though, for the regulatory regime to be as clear and unambiguous as possible (Brown, Stern, and Tenenbaum 2006).

Some DFIs can sometimes facilitate a form of credit support through what is known as the "A and B loan" structure: as several DFIs enjoy preferential lender status with governments, commercial banks may complement DFI lending to a particular project (the A loan) with their own loan to the project (the B loan)[3] and so enjoy the same preferred creditor protection as the DFI for that particular lending operation. For example, the IDB built the financial structure for the first phase of the São Paulo Metro Line 4 project around a direct 15-year A loan from the IDB to the concessionaire, accompanied by a syndicated 12-year B loan from various commercial project finance lenders.

The risk that the public authority will not meet its payment obligations is particularly relevant to projects in emerging markets that depend on long-term payments from government (such as availability-based PPPs). This is compounded by the fact that lenders may be expected to take the risk of multiannual budget approvals: What if the government does not approve the budget for a particular line ministry to enable it to pay the availability payment? This is one of the major obstacles to availability-based PPPs in emerging markets, especially if the payment constitutes a significant proportion of the budget for the authority. In Brazil, the federal government established a guarantee fund dedicated specifically to cover such a potential risk. While the federal government has a good record of servicing long-term debt obligations, confidence in long-term PPP contractual obligations had to be developed. The fund is not the primary source of payment under the PPP, but it is available if the public authority does not comply with its payment obligations. Specific reference is made to the fund in the underlying

---

[3] Cross-defaulted with the DFI's own participation in the B loan.

project contract. The federal government guarantee fund comprises various high-quality and transparently valued assets, such as government shares in quoted blue-chip companies, and is managed by a separate professional fund manager. The value of the fund must always be maintained in relation to the obligations covered. Several Brazilian and Mexican state governments have established similar funds for state government obligations under PPPs. This approach is also being considered by other countries. The long-term intention, however, is that, as market confidence in government develops, the need for such guarantees will diminish. This underlines one of the key themes in this guide: developing PPPs is as much about strategic approaches to developing the markets overall for PPP *programs* as it is about one-off project transactions.

Other Forms of Guarantees

Guarantees may also be provided by the public authority to cover specific project risks—a guarantee of minimum levels of traffic on a toll road, for example. In the São Paulo Metro Line 4 case study, for instance, the concessionaire benefits from a minimum revenue guarantee and revenue-sharing threshold, protecting it from lower than expected revenues, but providing the public authority with revenue sharing if use is higher than projected. The use of such guarantees needs to be evaluated and structured very carefully, as there are numerous examples where the transfer of such risks (and the resulting costs) to the public authority has created significant fiscal problems, often calling into question the rationale for the project to be structured as a PPP (Irwin 2007). Developing strong competition between funders wherever possible and ensuring access to good financial advice are important to ensure that the public authority does not find itself taking back project risks that it has already paid to transfer, thus destroying the incentives of the PPP mechanism and creating unsustainable fiscal obligations.

Other Sources of Funding

Where it may be difficult to raise long-term debt for the full amount required, the government itself may act as one of the long-term lenders to a project but still benefit from the discipline of having private sector capital at risk to performance. This has the advantage of creating the possibility of refinancing and recovering such funding in the future when markets are more open, while underpinning and giving confidence to the market when required. The disadvantage clearly is that the public authority assumes part of the risks normally transferred to the private sector, which may create a potential conflict of interest that needs to be resolved, and, of course, it requires public resources. However, if a significant part of the funding is still provided by the private sector, the disciplines of private sector capital at risk to performance are still available to drive the incentives required of the PPP structure. Governments such as France and the United Kingdom have from time to time used such approaches when required for their PPP programs.

Public Sector–Funded Development Banks

In many countries, especially emerging economies, the principal source of long-term funding may be public sector development banks. Such institutions may be set up specifically to work closely with commercial lenders, providing additional government-backed co-financing capacity (for example, the India Infrastructure Finance Company), or they might have their own internal capacity to assess and manage their loan portfolios (for example, Banco Nacional de Desenvolvimento Econômico e Social in Brazil [BNDES], the Banco Nacional de Obras y Servicios Publicos in Mexico [BANOBRAS], or Vnesheconombank in the Russian Federation). These may be important sources of stability and market development and, as institutions in their own right, may bring as much of the lender due diligence and monitoring disciplines as private sector lenders. Indeed, given their public mission, they may also be sources of further policy support and quality control in PPPs over and above those required by commercial lenders. DFIs, as publicly owned entities, fall into this category—the European Investment Bank, for example, has a portfolio of more than €25 billion of PPP projects across the European Union.[4]

Viability Gap Funding

The previous section describes various mechanisms for opening channels to private sources of long-term funding that might otherwise be closed and the role of direct government lending to projects. In some user-fee PPPs, the user tariff may be established by policy. This may be insufficient to generate a level of revenue over the life of the project to repay and reward the debt and equity funding if such funding were required to finance the *entire* capital costs of the project. In this case, the public authority may pay for part of the capital cost itself, thus reducing the amount of debt and equity funding required. This is sometimes known as a capital contribution. The PPP approach makes sense in such cases, as a substantial part of the capital costs still involve private capital at risk—the capital contribution simply makes the project financially viable when it might otherwise not be. An alternative method of making such a contribution on user-fee projects is to make payments during the operating phase, depending on

---

[4] www.eib.org, as of January 2009.

the availability performance of the project, which, alongside some level of payment from users, make up the overall revenue stream. This still requires the full capital costs to be financed, but it reduces or even eliminates the dependence of the project on tariff revenue, while strongly incentivizing operating performance.

An example of the capital contribution approach is India's viability gap funding (VGF) mechanism. The Viability Gap Fund, which is widely used by state governments for the substantial highways PPP program, makes available a maximum subsidy of 40 percent of the capital cost of the project—at most half of this can come from the central government's Viability Gap Fund, and the rest can be contributed by the sponsoring agency. (State governments have, outside of the VGF framework, gone beyond this level of support.) Such funding is normally disbursed pro rata, with the disbursements of debt and after the equity funding has been contributed to the project. As the road user toll (which is paid by the motorist) is broadly a fixed amount per kilometer across the program, private sector bidders bid the lowest VGF amount (as opposed to the lowest toll). The availability of the grant is based on strict conditionalities, such as the requirement for competitive bidding, central approval of the project, and use of standard concession terms wherever possible, helping to ensure quality control over the process. In the Republic of Korea, an extensive PPP program also has a mechanism for providing construction subsidies to qualifying projects. Some projects may combine this approach with availability-based payment schemes.

Output-Based Aid

Output-based aid (OBA) is an approach that seeks to make projects financially viable by subsidizing part of the payment for service delivery. This is especially targeted at the poorer sectors of the community that may not be able to pay the full tariff required to ensure the project's financial viability. A crucial element is that OBA payments are based on performance and only made to the private partner once a defined output has been achieved— for example, an electricity or water connection. Thus, unlike VGF, the full funding requirement for the project still needs to be raised. This is quite similar to an availability-based PPP, although a significant part of the project revenue comes directly from the users and the OBA payment usually only meets specific output-based requirements in the *early* stages of the project life cycle, phasing out over time. An example would be the cost of connecting a household to the water or power supply system, but not the supply of water or power itself. Long-term tariff revenue is usually (though not always) expected to cover at least operation and maintenance costs of the project. In the case of the Manila Water Company project (see the case study at the end of the chapter), OBA support is being used to fund part of the connection charges for up to 21,000 poorer households to be covered by the network, and the scheme has been embedded in an existing concession arrangement. OBA schemes can be effective in leveraging private investment in otherwise challenging infrastructure sectors that benefit the poor, unlocking some of the performance-based risk-sharing incentives of PPPs. They can encourage innovation and efficiency in service delivery by focusing on outputs, while ensuring greater transparency and better targeting of subsidies to those who need them most. Clearly the extent of OBA depends on the availability of resources from donors to fund the longer-term OBA payments. The challenges for successful OBA schemes are very similar to those for other forms of PPP: ensuring that the outputs are defined appropriately and that the subsidy is targeted and administered correctly. One of the principal OBA schemes is run by the Global Partnership on Output-based Aid (GPOBA), a partnership of donors and international organizations.[5]

---

[5] See www.gpoba.org.

Case Study: São Paulo Metro Line 4, Brazil

Project:	São Paulo Metro Line 4
Description:	30-year contract in which the public sector is responsible for construction of the Metro Line 4 in São Paulo, while the private sector is responsible for operation and maintenance as well as for the supply of trains and signaling and control systems
Financial close:	October 2008
Capital value:	US$392.15 million (phase 1), of which US$309.2 million is debt (15-year A loan from the IDB for US$69.2 million accompanied by a syndicated 12-year B loan for approximately US$240 million) and US$82.95 million is equity
Consortium:	ViaQuatro—Concessionaria da Linha 4 do Metro de São Paulo—comprising Companhia de Concessões Rodoviarias of Brazil (68 percent), Montgomery Participações of Portugal (30 percent), RATP Development of France (1 percent), and Benito Roggio Transportes of Argentina (1 percent)
Financiers:	Inter-American Development Bank, Banco Santander, Southern Missouri Bancorp, KfW, Banco Espírito Santo, BBVA, plus the involvement of Société Générale and West LB as coordinators

São Paulo is the largest city in Brazil and one of the most densely inhabited cities in the world. With intense traffic, the city continuously needs to expand its subway network to serve its growing population. São Paulo's modern metro system totals 61.3 kilometers in four lines and 55 stations. However, the network does not reach the outer suburbs of the metropolitan area.

In order to connect the central business district with key residential, medical, and university areas, the government of the State of São Paulo decided to add a new line to the state's existing metro network through a PPP scheme. The new line 4 (the "yellow line") will cross metropolitan São Paulo in a southwest-northeast direction and will integrate the subway with both the suburban rail system and the city's bus networks. With a total extension of approximately 12.8 kilometers, it will add about 21 percent of additional capacity to the metro network.

The project will be implemented in two phases. During phase 1, the Companhia do Metropolitano de São Paulo—the public authority that owns the underground network—will be responsible for constructing the tunneling, track, and metro stations. The private sector contractor, ViaQuatro, under a 30-year concession agreement, will be responsible for the supply, operation, and maintenance of the rolling stock (14 metro trains with six cars each) and operating systems (a train signaling and control system and a mobile voice and data communications system). During phase 1, according to the state's time frame, six stations will be built by the first quarter of 2010.

The second phase, which is subject to further studies and market demand, will require the private sector contractor to open additional stations on the existing line and add between five and 15 more trains, at the discretion of the State of São Paulo, at any time after the second year of commercial operations.

This project was not eligible for support from the Brazilian government's development bank, BNDES, because the trains are manufactured outside the country, mainly in the Republic of Korea (Hiundai), Italy (Roten), and Germany (Siemens). Therefore, public sector financing for construction of the tunnels was provided by the World Bank and the Japan Bank for International Cooperation, while financing for ViaQuatro, the private concessionaire, was led by the IDB. This project is a major achievement considering the challenging market conditions under which the deal was closed and the specific financing requirements of the concession.

A first complication was that the State of São Paulo required ViaQuatro to commit financing for both phases, although the timing, size, and even certainty of the second phase of the project were uncertain. In response to the two-phase obligation, the IDB built the financial structure around a two-phase loan framework. Phase 1 involved a direct 15-year A loan from the IDB to ViaQuatro of US$69.2 million, accompanied by a syndicated 12-year B loan for approximately US$240 million. Phase 2 would require a second A loan of US$59.5 million, and a B loan could be added, whose amount will be finalized once the investment program for phase 2 is defined by the government. The approach adopted by IDB reduces the financial risks for ViaQuatro, while the A/B loan umbrella of the IDB provides the flexibility to incorporate additional financing for phase 2.[6]

A second complicating factor is that the government is not obliged to complete the construction within its own identified time frame, that is, by

---

[6] http://idbdocs.iadb.org/wsdocs/getdocument.aspx?docnum=1296464.

the first quarter of 2010. What happens if it is late in completing the tunnel infrastructure? To mitigate this problem, the debt allows for some flexibility if the public authority does not deliver the public works on time. Although the two maturities are inclusive of the construction phase, at 12 and 15 years door-to-door, the interest-only grace period of the debt lasts as long as the actual period of tunnel construction. Principal repayments on both tranches only begin once the asset is in operation. If the construction phase takes two years, the principal repayments will be made over 10 years for the B loan and 13 years for the A loan. However, the longer the construction takes, the larger the installments, and the shorter the time to service the debt.[7]

As per the concession agreement, ViaQuatro will receive its revenues from the subway fare (set at US$1 for all trips), adjusted annually for inflation. It will receive 100 percent of the full fare for passengers using only Line 4 and 50 percent of the fare for passengers using Line 4 in connection with other metro and bus lines. In addition, ViaQuatro will receive yearly availability payments of US$44.1 million from the government and will be allowed to obtain alternative revenues by marketing spaces in the facilities and trains, as long as they do not affect the quality and standard of services. Finally, the concession benefits from a minimum revenue-guarantee and revenue-sharing threshold, protecting the concessionaire from low revenues, but providing the state with revenue sharing if use is higher than projections.

The concession agreement requires ViaQuatro to provide regular information on the development and performance of the project. For instance, before the expected start of operations of Line 4 in 2010, ViaQuatro needs to develop and effectively implement appropriate environmental, social, and health and safety management systems to ensure that operation and maintenance of Line 4 will be carried out within the appropriate standards and in compliance with Brazil's and the IDB's policies and requirements.

Furthermore, ViaQuatro will be assessed periodically based on three types of performance indicators: (a) operating performance indicators, (b) users' satisfaction indicators (which will be performed by an independent institution and will assess the level of satisfaction of users of the new line by means of specific direct surveys), and (c) maintenance quality indicators. If the values of these indicators fall below certain defined limits, ViaQuatro may be penalized through a reduction of its entitlement to income associated with the services provided.

---

[7] www.projectfinancemagazine.com.

As to social and environmental benefits, the project is expected to have a significant impact on living standards in São Paulo by reducing commuting time, road traffic, risk of accidents, and pollution.

The project offers the following key lessons:

- A key risk for the project is the interface between delivery of the publicly funded civil works and the rolling-stock PPP. A complex set of contractual obligations and financial arrangements was put in place to ensure that the private partner was compensated for any delays in provision of the public works. It is too soon to know how this will work in practice, but the project has demonstrated that investors are prepared to take key interface risks if they are structured properly.
- A key feature of the project is the allocation of risk. In this case, the allocation of risk associated with tunneling and track provision was considered better value for money if retained by the public sector, but other key risks, such as demand and operation as well as rolling-stock provision, were successfully shared with the private sector: the compensation arrangements for the private concessionaire can involve a mix of user-fee and availability-based payment mechanisms that reflect the detailed allocation of risk.
- An effective contract monitoring process is vital to ensure the delivery of high-quality public services and infrastructure. Availability of detailed contract performance data is crucial to determine both performance-based payments and deductions.
- DFIs can play an important role in helping to achieve financial close on large, complex PPPs in difficult and often unanticipated market conditions.

Case Study: Improved Access to Water Services in the East Zone of Metro Manila, the Philippines

Project:	Improved access to water services in the East Zone of Metro Manila
Description:	Four-year project to provide access to water services to individual households from the low-income communities of Antipolo City, Baras, Rodriguez, and San Mateo in Rizal Province and Taguig City
Financial close:	October 2007
Capital value:	US$17 million (including $1.05 million GPOBA grant)
Consortium:	Manila Water Company
Financiers:	Manila Water Company and Global Partnership on Output-based Aid (grant)

In the mid-1990s, metropolitan Manila had a very poor water supply service, as about 70 percent of the water supplied was lost and only a few areas in the metropolis had a 24-hour supply. Poor households had limited access to piped water, and many of them resorted to unregistered connections or water vendors to cover their needs. The water production and distribution assets were dilapidated, and it was not possible to cope with population growth.

To tackle these problems, in 1995 the government of the Philippines passed the National Water Crisis Act, which led to the involvement of the private sector in the provision of water and sewerage services in metropolitan Manila. In August 1997 the Manila Water Company (MWC) took over the operation of the East Zone of metropolitan Manila as concessionaire of the government-owned Metropolitan Waterworks and Sewerage System under a 25-year concession agreement.

Since 1997 MWC has met and exceeded its major service obligations and now serves more than 5.1 million people. The company has reduced nonrevenue water levels to around 25 percent and increased the coverage of 24-hour service to 98 percent of the area covered by its network. MWC has also regularized unregistered service connections and provided new service connections to poor households through a program called "Tubig para sa Barangay" (Water for Your Community). Under this program, MWC paid for investment in the network, and households paid for the service connection through an installment plan. However, with time, MWC saw that the poorer households could not afford to pay the connection fee in full. A subsidy was needed to achieve universal access, and the GPOBA project provided a solution.

GPOBA decided to build on and deepen MWC's successful service expansion program to low-income communities and thus contribute to creating broader public and political support for private sector involvement in critical infrastructure services. This support remains fragile given the diverse track record of private concessions in Manila (such as the bankruptcy of the West Zone concessionaire, now rehabilitated) and the Philippines more broadly.

The objective of the GPOBA project is to provide access to water services to individual households from the low-income communities of Antipolo City, Baras, Rodriguez, and San Mateo in Rizal Province and Taguig City.

OBA Mechanism

The project is embedded in a larger network expansion effort by MWC, as stipulated in its five-year investment plan. The potential beneficiaries are approximately 21,000 poor households. In the absence of a national means-tested system for households or individuals, "community-based targeting" through surveys conducted by MWC to assess income levels against the national capital region poverty line was used to target the subsidies. The approximate per capita income of the targeted population is around US$300 a year.

The total project cost approximately US$17 million, with MWC investing US$14 million in new water supply infrastructure in the project areas. The total connection charge per household amounted to ₱7,531.73 (US$167). Each household contributed ₱1,620 (US$36), and GPOBA provided a subsidy for the remaining ₱5,911.73 (US$131). In order to make the household contribution more affordable, MWC proposed and is currently offering an installment scheme of payments over 36 months. The GPOBA subsidy will be paid directly to the MWC as a single payment, conditional on the independent verification of three months of satisfactory service delivery.

Results Achieved So Far

As of June 30, 2009, a total of 10,642 connections had been completed. Disbursements were delayed, however, due to difficulties in verifying compliance with water pressure output. The Manila Water Company has now provided pressure maps so that the output can be verified independently, and disbursement will proceed shortly.

Key Lessons

It is important for the recipient of OBA support to understand that outputs have to be delivered according to the agreed standards. This is a basic element of any OBA project, but as the decisive element for disbursement, it cannot be overemphasized.

Training should be provided in advance on implementing performance-based payment schemes. A dry run may be advisable.

A core team should be dedicated to project implementation. High rotation of staff has been a problem so far in the MWC project. A good mix of technical and financial staff should be part of the team.

Following successful implementation of the first stage of the project, several aspects of the scheme's design are under review. In particular, MWC has observed that many beneficiary households have not modified their water consumption patterns following connection; they continue to fill water containers for use inside their homes. As a result, some of the planned benefits of an individual household connection to a network of potable water supply are not materializing.

MWC has proposed an alternative design that involves providing beneficiary households with the internal plumbing necessary to bring the water to a kitchen sink and toilet. This arrangement, while improving access to water supply services, would significantly increase the volume of wastewater produced by each household. Many of the poorer communities lack facilities for the collection and treatment of wastewater. Thus GPOBA and MWC are working on a proposal to develop a comprehensive design incorporating wastewater management.

6.

PREPARING PROJECTS FOR MARKET

Chapter 4 looks at some of the key criteria in assessing and therefore selecting projects eligible for a public-private partnership (PPP). Once the initial selection has taken place, the focus moves to preparing the project for market. This may be considered the second main step in the project preparation process, as one moves from the "strategic business case" discussed in chapter 4 to what is sometimes referred to as the "outline business case." The term "final business case" then refers to the state of the project just before signature of the project agreement, discussed in chapter 9.

The project preparation phase at this point has two major aspects. First is the activity of ensuring that the public sector is adequately prepared and organized to manage the process. This activity is likely to include greater use of external advisers and consideration of budgets to fund the work. Second is the parallel activity of completing the full project assessment to ensure that the project is being developed on a sound basis. The activities at this stage require the public authority to undertake the following:

- Identify and assemble the project team, including advisers
- Establish the public sector's requirements for the project based on agreed policy, in accordance with the existing regulatory framework if relevant, and in a way that can be clearly articulated in contractual terms to potential public sector bidders
- Develop a high level of confidence in the potential level of private sector interest in the project, on the terms envisaged
- Determine what type of public sector support will be required (for example, provide part of the project funding, make assets such as land available, or make the payments for the service affordable)

- Confirm that the public sector can deliver on its obligations over the life of the project
- Develop a comprehensive and credible PPP contract and establish the basis for its operation, such as how disputes will be handled and the extent to which it is fixed or negotiable
- Develop the project information for bidders
- Identify all of the relevant statutory processes and clearances (environmental, access to land)
- Identify and consult the various project stakeholders[1]
- Develop a strategy for raising awareness of the project among potential investors
- Prepare for the procurement phase (strategy, budgets, timetable, and people)
- Complete the value-for-money assessments and establish the basis on which a project's success will be evaluated.

These tasks must be accomplished *before* private sector bidders are invited to spend serious time and effort considering the proposal. The activities are directly relevant to the project information that will eventually be made available to the private sector, as discussed in chapter 8, and they affect the credibility of the process when engaging with the private sector. See figure 6.1 for the elements of the project preparation process.

These various requirements must be kept in balance: increasing the scope of the project may be deliverable, but not affordable, or allocating certain risks may appear affordable and in line with requirements, but not be deliverable by the private partner. The outline business case is therefore a useful tool to bring all the elements together, so that any conflicts between these factors can be resolved before approaching the private sector. This document can be used to form the basis on which the project is assessed and approved for commencement of the procurement phase.

Management of the Process

Good governance and good project management, along with risk mitigation and quality control, are essential elements of managing a successful PPP process.

---

[1] Stakeholders are the various parties affected by the PPP project—not just the public authority or the private party, but, in a toll road, for example, road users, those who live near or may be displaced by the road, municipalities whose local traffic will be affected by it, and so on.

Figure 6.1   Project Preparation Process

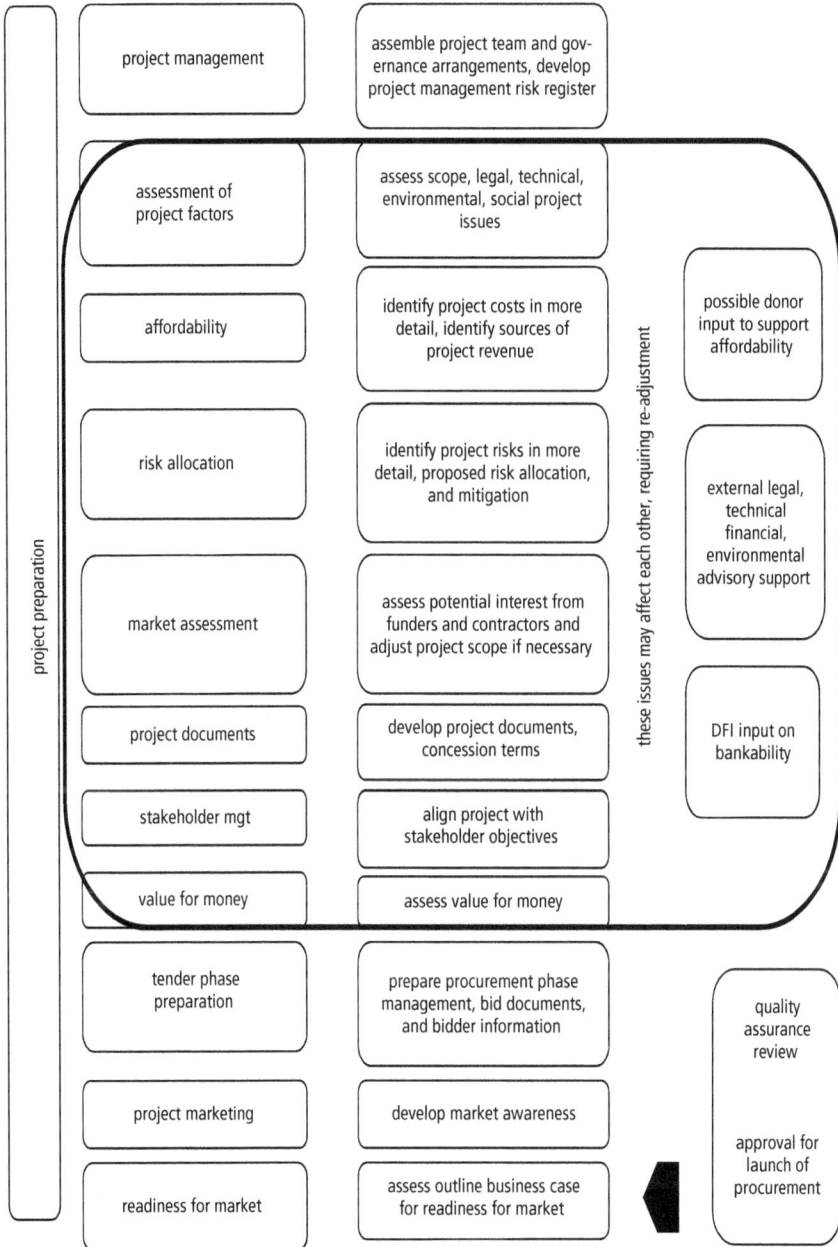

The flowchart shows the project preparation process organized as a vertical sequence:

project preparation (left side label spanning the process)

project management	assemble project team and governance arrangements, develop project management risk register
assessment of project factors	assess scope, legal, technical, environmental, social project issues
affordability	identify project costs in more detail, identify sources of project revenue
risk allocation	identify project risks in more detail, proposed risk allocation, and mitigation
market assessment	assess potential interest from funders and contractors and adjust project scope if necessary
project documents	develop project documents, concession terms
stakeholder mgt	align project with stakeholder objectives
value for money	assess value for money
tender phase preparation	prepare procurement phase management, bid documents, and bidder information
project marketing	develop market awareness
readiness for market	assess outline business case for readiness for market

Right-side annotations:
- possible donor input to support affordability
- external legal, technical financial, environmental advisory support
- DFI input on bankability
- quality assurance review
- approval for launch of procurement

(vertical label across the boxed group: these issues may affect each other, requiring re-adjustment)

Source: Authors.

Project Governance

Managing the preparation, procurement, and operation of a PPP project involves dealing with multiple issues with stakeholders all at the same time. Later in the procurement phase, it involves approving complex decisions, often with quite short timelines, while negotiating with private sector bidders who are likely to be highly organized and purposeful. During the construction and operation phases, it involves dealing with changes in the project, users, unforeseen events, and termination. Good project governance lies at the heart of successful delivery of the project and management of the interaction with the private sector.

In the early stage of project selection (discussed in chapter 4), governance structures may be quite fluid and simple. However, at the end of this phase or when a decision is made to devote more resources to the project, it is important to develop a more comprehensive structure of project governance (see figure 6.2).

A common way of implementing effective project governance is through a system of boards. A project board normally comprises the main public sector stakeholders and often, as a matter of good practice, independent members capable of providing neutral challenge, informed by technically sound experience; this is the regular forum for resolving key issues and for making decisions above the powers delegated to the project management team. It sets the project requirements, constraints, and boundaries, monitors the project management activities, and provides a forum for challenging and supporting the project team. Key project advisers are usually not project board members, but they may be called to attend meetings of the project board when expert advice needs to be examined firsthand.

For significant projects, it is helpful to identify a senior officer within the public authority, sometimes called the "project owner," who has ultimate responsibility for delivering the project and is capable, available, and willing to show leadership and commitment. This person may chair the project board. The project board may, in turn, report to a program-level board within the procuring authority if a significant program of projects is involved.

A full-time project director or manager is responsible for managing the project management team and reporting to the project board. The project team comprises functional managers drawn from across the public authority and deals with day-to-day management of the project within the delegated responsibility and authority. This also includes managing the project advisers. For complex projects, separate boards covering specific issues, such as wider stakeholder management, may be set up and report to the

Figure 6.2 Outline of a Structure of Project Governance

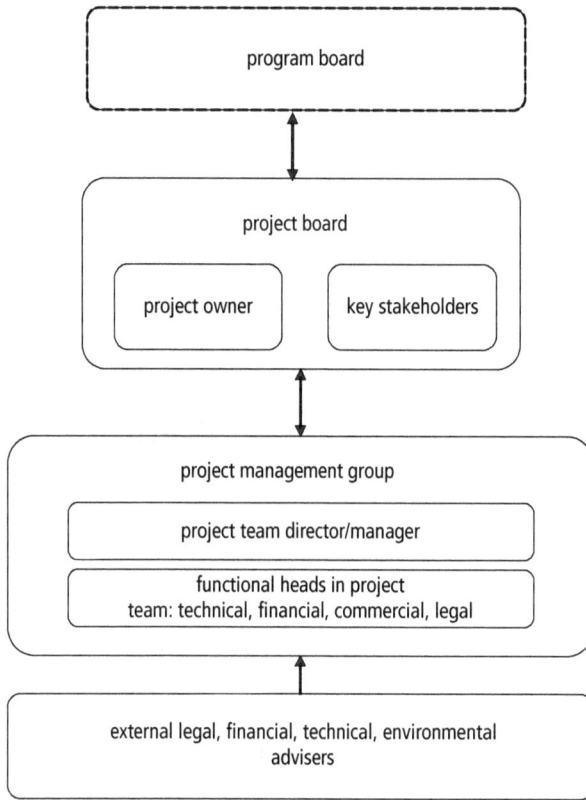

```
┌ ─ ─ ─ ─ ─ ─ ─ ─ ─ ─ ─ ─ ─ ─ ─ ─ ─ ─ ─ ─ ┐
│              program board               │
└ ─ ─ ─ ─ ─ ─ ─ ─ ─ ─ ─ ─ ─ ─ ─ ─ ─ ─ ─ ─ ┘
                    ↕
┌──────────────────────────────────────────┐
│              project board               │
│  ┌──────────────┐    ┌─────────────────┐ │
│  │ project owner│    │ key stakeholders│ │
│  └──────────────┘    └─────────────────┘ │
└──────────────────────────────────────────┘
                    ↕
┌──────────────────────────────────────────┐
│          project management group        │
│  ┌────────────────────────────────────┐  │
│  │   project team director/manager    │  │
│  ├────────────────────────────────────┤  │
│  │     functional heads in project    │  │
│  │ team: technical, financial, commercial, legal │
│  └────────────────────────────────────┘  │
└──────────────────────────────────────────┘
                    ↑
┌──────────────────────────────────────────┐
│ external legal, financial, technical, environmental │
│                  advisers                │
└──────────────────────────────────────────┘
```

Source: Authors.

project board. The project team may draw resources from a central PPP unit (discussed in chapter 3), a member of which might also be on the project board.

When establishing the project's governance structure, it is vital that project advocacy lies outside the project team. A senior champion within the public authority is needed, and the absence of one is often cited as a reason for projects to falter.

Stakeholder management is also a major activity of both the project team and the project board; failing to achieve the buy-in of stakeholders until late in the process and then trying to convince them of the merits of previous decisions is a recipe for delay. In the early phases of a PPP program, this may

Common Problems in Project Governance

- A part-time project manager (that is, someone who has another full-time job inside the public authority) and limited resourcing of the project team
- Loss of continuity and knowledge through badly managed or frequent changes in the project team
- Lack of resources, including advisers, or, conversely, excessive reliance on advisers for decision making
- Insufficient delegation of powers to the project management group so that even the smallest decision needs to be referred upward
- Interference from other bodies outside the governance structure so that no one knows who is actually running the day-to-day operations
- Poor management of the day-to-day resources, including the external advisers
- A project board that is too large and unable to meet as required to make key decisions.

be especially important, as it can often entail convincing the public sector to accept that the project will involve private sector management of what has typically been a public sector activity (see box 6.1 for a list of common governance problems).

Program Management

Above the project level, *program* management may offer additional benefits. For instance, the case study at the end of this chapter shows that, by adopting a PPP program approach in the national highways sector, rather than an ad hoc individual project approach, the Indian government has generated benefits such as standardization and more consistent delivery of projects than might otherwise have been the case.

Adopting a program management approach brings the following benefits:

- Improving the management and coordination of the pipeline of projects and the matching of supply to demand
- Enabling effective communication of policy to the market
- Improving the participation of stakeholders
- Building market confidence and supply-side capacity

- Shaping the market to create newer, deeper supply capability
- Reducing transaction costs through replicability and greater use of standardization
- Leveraging public sector bulk purchasing power in relation to risk transfer negotiations
- Enabling the development of programwide quality-assurance processes.

Use of a Risk Management Matrix

A good project management practice is to establish a matrix of risks that applies to the project preparation process itself. This identifies who does what, whether budgets are in place, and how risks will be mitigated. The matrix changes at different stages in the cycle. An extract example can be seen in appendix B. This is not the same as the risk matrix used to identify the allocation of risks within the project itself, which is a separate exercise (see chapter 4).

Quality Control

PPP programs around the world also use quality-assurance mechanisms for good project and program management. These can be short external reviews to help the public authority to check that the necessary actions have been taken at important decision-making points in the PPP project development cycle. These would usually be (a) before significant expenditure of resources on project preparation is undertaken (that is, at the conclusion of the strategic business case stage), (b) before going to market (at the conclusion of the outline business case stage), (c) before entering into the long-term agreement (at the final business case stage), and (d) at some point in the operations phase to examine if project benefits are being achieved. For example, just prior to launching the procurement, a review will check, among other things, that the project's outputs are still aligned with the original requirements, that the correct project management structures are in place to manage the next phase, and that market capacity and interest exist for the project. Such a review can usually be carried out in a few days and therefore should not hold up the process. This activity is not necessarily an audit, but a source of constructive challenge for the public authority to ensure that the project is ready to proceed to the next stage. An example is the project "gateway" process that is widely used across the public sector in the United Kingdom (United Kingdom, Office of Government Commerce 2007) and several other countries such as Australia and the Netherlands. This process can capture many of the issues that may otherwise trip up a project later on and promotes consistency in approach. See box 6.2 for common mistakes in project preparation.

Common Mistakes in Project Preparation

- Lack of clarity by the public authority regarding what it wants from the project
- Lack of project ownership and leadership
- Poorly resourced project (and program) teams
- Selection of advisers on the basis of cost rather than quality and experience
- Lack of effective engagement with stakeholders
- Lack of understanding of and contact with the private sector at senior levels and poorly conducted market sounding
- Expectations that the private sector will deal with issues, such as the acquisition of land, that are better handled by the public sector
- Lack of clarity about the public authority's legal powers to enter into the public-private partnership contract
- Conflict between the procurement process and procurement regulations
- Overly ambitious project preparation timetables
- Release of incomplete project information.

Funding for Project Preparation

The up-front costs of project preparation and tendering should not be underestimated. These costs may typically be 3–4 percent of investment costs for projects costing less than US$100 million, 2–3 percent for projects costing more than US$100 million, and around 2 percent for projects costing more than US$500 million (excluding significant costs of land, early works, and environmental impact assessments). As such costs may be disproportionately high in such cases, small one-off projects are not generally suited to PPPs.

In many regions, development finance institutions (DFIs) and donor organizations have established facilities to help pay for the costs of project preparation, although fewer such facilities are available for upstream framework-setting activities. An example of the latter is the Public-Private Infrastructure Advisory Facility (PPIAF) managed by the World Bank.

Another approach to mobilizing resources for project development is for the government to establish and manage a revolving project development fund, possibly with donor support. The winning bidders effectively refinance such costs at contract signing, recycling funds back to other public authorities. An example of such a fund is the South African Treasury's PPP

Project Development Facility (South Africa, National Treasury 2004a). This approach can also provide some discipline, consistency, and quality control in the appointment of advisers.

Apart from direct funding, DFIs can also play a valuable, although more informal, role as a sounding board throughout project development (see chapter 8).

Unsolicited Proposals

Private companies often approach governments directly with new project ideas, typically referred to as unsolicited proposals. Such proposals can introduce innovative ideas and contribute to infrastructure goals where governments have limited capacity to develop projects. This may be the case particularly at the local or municipal levels of government. However, this approach, if handled badly, can raise issues of transparency, serve special interests, suppress competition, and deliver poor value for money. For these reasons, some governments disallow unsolicited proposals, while others seek to channel such proposals into a transparent, competitive process that encompasses many of the same disciplines used to review projects generated by the public sector but also requires the private sector proponent to develop the detailed proposal. The subsequent process then involves a competitive tender, where the original proponent may have an additional theoretical value attached to its bid or have the right to match a better offer or to participate in a final round of bidding. The challenge is to manage the risks that such unsolicited proposals involve for the public interest (Do the projects really meet a public investment need?) and ensure that there is a genuinely effective competitive process (Is there sufficient time for alternative credible bids to be prepared?).

Given that project proponents are encouraged to develop (at their cost) and put forward project proposals, unsolicited bids are sometimes regarded as a source of funding for project development. However, the original proponent usually expects these costs to be reimbursed if the project is awarded to another party. While these costs may be funded out of the financing structure of the eventual project (the public sector or user will ultimately pay for them), there can be issues in determining how to assess and control such costs and how to discourage frivolous project proposals, all of which require government capacity to manage the process in the first place. The public sector will still incur costs related to analyzing the proposals and running the procurement process itself (see, for example, Hodges and Dellacha 2007). Thus unsolicited proposals do not take the burden of capacity off the public sector as much as might at first appear. There are still benefits to this approach, however, as it can sometimes give rise to new approaches to infrastructure delivery, but the risks and potential costs need to be examined realistically and managed carefully.

Project Assessment

Assessing the various factors that affect the scope, affordability, risk allocation, value for money, and contract development of a project involves a variety of skills. After the project selection phase, this work becomes much more intense. The allocation of activities and the steps they involve can usefully be described with regard to diverse disciplines involved at this stage.

Legal and Regulatory Assessment

This step seeks to assess the issues that are internal to the public authority. In particular, it seeks to assure that there are no legal impediments to the public authority entering into the various project agreements and that the procurement process envisaged is legal. This is important to ensure that proper procedures are followed and to minimize the risk of challenge—for example, from unsuccessful bidders that may derail the process. Project-specific issues will also arise, including assessment of the legal status of the various project assets or rights required (for example, land use or title). In the case of refurbishment projects, the private sector needs to understand the condition of the existing assets, the proposed handling of historical liabilities, and the availability and value of any indemnities.

The legal assessment also covers the relationship between the public authority and the project and between the project and other relevant parties—that is, issues that may be considered external to the authority. For example, the drawing up of project requirements and the identification and allocation of risks need to be reflected properly in the draft PPP contract through the output specifications, payment mechanism provisions, and other terms of the contract. The legal team also needs to develop other key components of the PPP contract, including provisions for resolving disputes and mechanisms for governing changes in the project.

Many PPP projects are highly dependent on other facilities. For example, a thermal power-generating facility depends on reliable transport infrastructure for its supply of fuel feedstock and on transmission infrastructure for its power off-take. Confirmation of the status and availability of such infrastructure is required, reflected in the terms and conditions of the associated agreements. The creditworthiness of the counterparties (that is, the bankability of these agreements) is significant to the commercial viability of the project. Private sector investors are reluctant to spend time assessing a project's viability unless these issues are well defined in legal terms. This can be a significant component of project preparation.

A well-developed and comprehensive suite of project documents, especially those that involve the public authority, will need to be made available to private sector bidders during the procurement process. The time to prepare these documents is *before* the procurement phase is launched. Depending on the procurement process used, the eventual terms in these agreements, including the allocation of some of the risks, may well change as a result of the interaction with the market. However, a realistic allocation of risks and contractual terms must be established at the start of the process to engage the interest of serious bidders and enhance the credibility of the public sector and the project. This process may start at a high level, when making a strategic case for the project (see chapter 4), but will then be looked at in much more detail during the preparation of the outline business case.

Technical, Social, and Environmental Assessment

The technical assessment determines whether the project's output requirements are technically feasible and estimates the likely capital and operating expenditure required. Specific initial work on ground and hydrographical conditions and even archeological surveys may be required. Designs to a reasonable level of detail may be developed in certain projects, not necessarily to instruct bidders, but to illustrate how the output requirements may be interpreted (sometimes referred to as a "design protocol") and to support estimates of the likely project costs for the affordability assessment. There may also be an insurance review at this stage to assess the likelihood of transferring risk to the insurance markets, the expected costs, and the availability of insurance cover.

An important component of the technical assessment is an analysis of environmental and social issues to ensure that there are no adverse impacts to impede delivery of the project. This involves identifying any potential environmental and social risks and looking at how such risks can be mitigated to ensure compliance with legal requirements or environmental policies (possibly by changing the scope of the project, such as amending the alignment of a road). Many project lenders, especially DFIs and banks adopting the Equator Principles,[2] will only lend if strict environmental conditions are met. If DFI funding is likely to be needed, then it is important to anticipate the requirements in this regard. This avoids having to repeat environmental and social impact studies and, at worst, having to change the scope of the project later to meet the criteria of DFIs or other lenders.

---

[2] A set of principles, developed by the World Bank, covering environmental and social protection eligibility lending criteria.

Financial Assessment

Financial assessment involves various activities. First, by bringing together the various elements of project cost referred to above, it enables an analysis of the expected long-term project revenue requirements, which are particularly relevant to the affordability analysis. This analysis estimates the expected level and conditions of debt and equity funding required and the exposure to inflation, long-term currency mismatch, or interest rate movements. All of these may have a major impact on whether the private sector can finance and deliver the project as well as on the structure of the PPP contract.

Case Study: PPP Program in the National Highways Sector, India

Project: National Highways Development Project (NHDP)

Description: A seven-phase development program largely, though not exclusively, involving private participation in the development, maintenance, and operation of national highways. The first two phases of the program are near completion. The subsequent phases envisage six lanes of 6,500 kilometers, four lanes of 17,500 kilometers, upgrading of 20,000 kilometers of national highways, and initiation of work on 1,000 kilometers of expressways.

With 3.3 million kilometers, India has the second largest road network in the world. Out of this, national highways account for only 2 percent of the total length but share almost 40 percent of the total passenger and freight traffic on India's roads. Until 1999, road construction and maintenance activities were financed largely through the government budget and borrowings from multilateral agencies. However, financial resources for the sector were inadequate, which resulted in the addition of minimal capacity, low maintenance, and ultimately poor-quality roads. Lack of investment in the highways infrastructure has been recognized as one of the key constraints to economic growth and competitiveness. The National Highways Development Project, India's largest highways program, was developed as a specific policy response to this issue, a significant component of which envisaged the mobilization of private sector skills and resources.[3]

At the policy level, a committee on infrastructure, chaired by the prime minister, was created to formulate and implement the necessary central government policies for PPPs, including their use in the highways sector. The committee oversees the selection of priority programs and projects appropriate for PPPs, the initiation of structures that maximize the efficient use of PPPs, the monitoring of projects, and the production and dissemination of guidelines on how to finance, formulate, appraise, approve, and implement PPPs.[4]

---

[3] http://www.nhai.org/WHATITIS.asp.
[4] http://infrastructure.gov.in.

At the institutional level, a central government sector–focused agency, the National Highways Authority of India (NHAI), was created to develop and manage delivery of the NHDP and to implement PPP structures for highways in line with PPP policy, where the use of PPPs is deemed appropriate.[5]

At a legislative level, the National Highways Act was amended to allow private sector entities to build, operate, and maintain national highways for specified periods and to levy fees to recover costs and generate reasonable returns. Furthermore, foreign direct investment up to 100 percent of equity was permitted and concession periods of up to 30 years were facilitated. A standardized detailed model concession agreement was developed together with procurement documents to award PPP projects within a competitive and transparent framework. The model concession agreement covers key issues such as risk mitigation and allocation, symmetry of obligations and rewards between parties, predictability of costs and obligations, reduction of transaction costs, force majeure, and termination. It also deals with other important investor concerns such as user protection. A manual of specifications and standards defines the technical parameters of design, construction, operation, and maintenance for two-, four-, and six-lane national highways to which the private sector contractor must conform. Equally, the standardized documentation and process for procurement seek to provide transparent and fair bidding procedures; and a financial support mechanism involving the allocation, through a competitive bid process, of viability gap funding from the government was developed to permit the financial viability of projects within a regime that involves a nationally established per kilometer road-user fee.

The NHAI has adopted a seven-phase program approach: the earlier phases, comprising around 6,000 kilometers linking four principal cities (Delhi, Mumbai, Chennai, and Kolkata) and 7,300 kilometers of north-south and east-west corridors, are nearing completion. These initial phases were funded mostly with public resources (financed through a fee on petroleum and diesel). However, subsequent phases of the NHDP (phases 3 to 7) involve a major role for the private sector, with the bulk of the projects to be implemented under concession PPP (toll-based) schemes. As part of its role, NHAI is required to purchase land and deliver to the concessionaire the necessary alignments free of encumbrances. Fiscal incentives, such as duty-free imports of high-capacity, modern construction equipment and 100 percent tax exemption for a period of 10 years in a block of 20 years, also seek to improve financial returns on investment.

---

[5] http://www.nhai.org.

It is still too early to assess the overall effectiveness of the PPP element of the program for risk transfer and operations, as many of the projects have only recently commenced operations and many are still in construction.

The program, however, offers the following key lessons:

- Identifying a national sector program, rather than ad hoc individual projects, can generate benefits for the consistency, quality, and, potentially, speed of delivery of projects. The program approach can also help both the public and private sectors to plan better to meet the demand over time. This can help to create a more competitive response from the market.
- Developing national and sector-specific agencies to deliver sector investment programs can facilitate faster and more coordinated delivery of projects and help to recycle experience within the public sector (although high staff turnover within an agency may mitigate this).
- Handling programwide legislative amendments, responsive to sector requirements, can lead to more consistency and thus a more effective policy and market response.
- Use of a standardized concession and procurement documentation model can improve the quality of concession terms and help to ensure greater transparency and consistency of the bidding process.
- Over time, the NHAI should be better placed to manage ongoing PPP projects robustly and to analyze and review the rollout of the program, making in-flight adjustments to the policy and program as necessary. Review of a program is doubly important to ensure that potentially ineffective programwide terms or processes are identified quickly and rectified.

7.

PROJECT ADVISERS

It would be unusual for the project team to have all the necessary specialist skills available internally. Professional advisers should be used where their skills will add value to the project's preparation, procurement, and management activities, but the objectives and leadership of the project should remain the public sector's responsibility. Gaps in skills should be identified at the outset, and options should be considered for securing any additional resources required. As part of their appointment, advisers should be required to transfer their skills to the project team (for example, by preparing guidance notes or providing training at the conclusion of an assignment). Where the governments are new to public-private partnerships (PPPs), they may need external advice to assist them in identifying which external advisers to hire, what sort of advice they can expect to obtain, and where they can obtain assistance in developing the terms of reference for these advisers and even in managing the interface with the various advisers. International financial institutions and other development agencies can assist governments in considering their options.[1]

Role of Advisers

The primary role of advisers is to give the project management group appropriate advice in their area of expertise. External advisers likely to be required for a PPP project will usually include a technical adviser, a financial adviser, a legal adviser, an environmental adviser, and, in countries with limited PPP experience, a lead transaction adviser (see table 7.1). Other specialists, such as social impact, insurance, accounting, and tax advisers, may also be required.

---

[1] For a more detailed discussion on the topic of this chapter, see World Bank and PPIAF (2001).

Table 7.1 Role of External Advisers

Type of adviser	Role
Lead transaction adviser	Assist government to coordinate the work of all advisers and manage the interface between government officials and the other advisers (may be relevant for countries new to PPPs)
Technical adviser	Support the development and feasibility of the technical aspects of the strategic plan and outline business cases
	Draft the project output requirements and specifications
	Develop payment mechanisms in conjunction with the financial advisers
	Ensure that all technical aspects of the project meet the objectives
	Evaluate and advise on all technical solutions throughout the procurement phase
	Scrutinize the costs of the bidders' solutions throughout the procurement phase
	Undertake technical due diligence on bidders' solutions
	Carry out any site condition, planning, and design work
	Provide support in the clarification and fine-tuning of technical issues
Financial adviser	Support the development of the financial aspects of the project's business case, in particular, the appraisal of different options, financial modeling, and input on bankable finance terms
	Develop project payment mechanisms in conjunction with the technical advisers
	Prepare the requirements for submitting a financial bid
	Ensure that all financial aspects of the bidders' solutions meet the requirements for submitting a financial bid
	Optimize and scrutinize the financial models submitted by bidders
	Evaluate and advise on all financial proposals throughout the procurement phase
	Review the funding, accounting, and taxation aspects of solutions proposed
	Undertake financial due diligence on bids submitted
	Provide support in the clarification and fine-tuning of financial and commercial issues

(continued next page)

Table 7.1 Role of External Advisers *(Continued)*

Type of adviser	Role
Legal adviser	Assist the public authority in assessing the requisite powers and legal feasibility of the project
	Develop the contract documentation for the project
	Develop other legal aspects of bid documents, including analysis of the project's assets, land ownership, interface agreements, and other site-related issues
	Ensure that bids meet legal and contractual requirements
	Evaluate and advise on all processes and legal and contractual solutions throughout the procurement phase and minimize the risk of bid challenge
	Undertake legal due diligence on bids
	Provide support in the clarification and fine-tuning of legal aspects
Environmental adviser	Examine the potential environmental impact of the project
	Identify the potential risks
	Consider risk mitigation measures and impact on scope and design of the project

Source: Authors.

When to Use Advisers

Advisers typically are involved at each stage of a PPP project:

- *The prefeasibility phase.* Advisers may assist in preparing the prefeasibility analysis, helping to determine the strategic investment case, the studies that may need to be commissioned, what questions to ask in the feasibility studies, whether the existing legal framework might allow the project to be developed as a PPP, and other basic parameters in which projects can be developed and implemented.
- *The initial feasibility assessment.* Advisers may assist in framing the outline proposals for procurement in the form of a commercial deal that can be taken to both contractors and the funding market. As part of this process, advisers should provide advice regarding what the funding market can be expected to deliver, the key constraints on the deal, and insight into the appetite of the market.
- *Development of the deal.* Advisers may assist in developing the detailed deal, including development of documentation such as the draft contract,

payment and performance mechanisms, allocation of risks between parties, financial models and other projections, and environmental assessment. Advisers can also assist in developing areas of tender documentation.

- *Execution of the deal.* Advisers may participate in the clarification and evaluation of bids. They may assist in negotiating the deal and providing analysis (legal, financial, technical, and environmental) on the implications of the positions adopted by the parties to the deal. This assistance may include advice on the optimum funding route and the timing and method of approaching the funding markets.
- *Construction and operation monitoring.* Advisers may also play a role during the operational phase, especially assisting in complex issues that may arise, such as refinancing or dealing with changes in the contract. They can also assist in monitoring compliance of the private sector with the terms of the contracts.

Appointment of Advisers

The competitive process for selecting advisers should aim to secure the best-quality and best-value advice. It is important to define the scope of work as closely as possible before contracting with advisers. In addition to considerations of cost, the selection of advisers ideally should involve an assessment of the depth and relevance of their expertise, their willingness and ability to access experience from other PPP markets if necessary, their capacity and willingness to provide advice relevant to the local conditions, their understanding of the project and the procuring authority's requirements and processes, and information regarding the availability of individuals who will do the work. The experience of the individuals put forward can often be more important than the reputation of the firm itself. The scope of work should set out clear milestones of advice at which point clear deliverables are to be provided by the advisers before payments are made. Fee arrangements should be set out clearly, specifying any assumptions that have been made to establish fixed-fee or cap arrangements together with any specific rules regarding expenses and travel. If input from particular individuals or a certain level of expertise are required, it is important to specify a minimum quantity of this expected input or expertise. If a particular individual is to travel internationally, this should also be specified.[2] In some markets, advisers may be appointed for the project preparation phase only and then

---

[2] Sample terms of reference for various advisers on PPPs can be found on the World Bank and PPIAF's PPP in Infrastructure Resource Center for Contracts, Laws, and Regulation at www.worldbank.org/pppiresource.

reappointed (or not) for the bidding phase of the project; this provides an opportunity to reassess their performance.

Role of Public-Private Partnership Units

Advisory support can be costly, and it is important for the public sector to be a sophisticated procurer and customer of external advisers. Their services should be used in a focused way to maximize their effectiveness and value. In countries where they have a track record of experience in undertaking transactions, PPP units can play a useful role in supporting the project team in the hiring and use of external expertise. This role can include offering advice on which advisers should be approached, the selection, appointment, and contracting process, and the terms of reference against which advisers should bid for the advisory mandate. PPP units often develop guidance in this respect and even become involved in the approval process (especially if they are managing the funding mechanisms for project development). By developing a more coordinated and consistent approach to the market, the government can help to encourage and develop the supply of good-quality advisers.

Management of Advisers

It is essential to give professional advisers sufficient access to the public authority's planning, deal development, management, and decision-making processes for them to understand the project's objectives and constraints and thus provide the best advice. It is counterproductive not to involve advisers fully in these aspects of a project, as this runs the risk that they will not have a complete picture and will give poor advice as a result. Advisers are not paid to agree with their clients; they are paid to offer professional, objective advice within their area of expertise.

Regular meetings should be held with advisers to discuss their reports, monitor their performance, enable them to account for their activity in a project, and discuss the issues faced.

In addition to regular meetings, it is good discipline to require advisers to sign off formally at key stages of a project, indicating that the project is ready to proceed to the next stage and that the proposals and timetable are realistic and deliverable. This encourages advisers to exercise due care and attention. If advisers do not believe that the project is ready to proceed, their objections should be formally recorded as well.

During the initial planning stages, project teams should budget appropriately for the cost of advisers throughout the process. A PPP unit can advise on the realistic costs of using advisers based on the complexity and size of the deal in question. While advisers' fees may seem expensive, in the context of deals that can exceed hundreds of millions of dollars in value, it is a false economy not to spend sufficient resources to ensure the availability of appropriate, high-quality advice.

The appointment of a lead or transaction adviser who then subcontracts and manages the other advisers can simplify the procurement process and reduce the burden on the public authority, which only has to manage one adviser. This would be particularly useful in countries that are just starting their PPP program. However, hiring a consortium of advisers can sometimes deny access to the most appropriate advisers in *each* area of expertise. In more mature PPP markets, advisers are generally appointed separately for this reason. An alternative procedure to avoid this pitfall would be to appoint advisers separately, but to include in this process the choice of an adviser whose terms of reference would be to assist in managing the interface of the government with the other advisers.

In the case of the rehabilitation and extension of the Queen Alia Airport (see the case study at the end of this chapter), the International Finance Corporation (IFC) acted as lead adviser to the Jordanian government, while also providing long-term financing to the project. In this instance, strong controls existed to ensure that there was no conflict of interest between the IFC's advising and lending activities and that the project benefited from the lender's clear knowledge of the sources and terms of finance. The case study also illustrates the role of an adviser in coordinating the various sources of advisory support and in developing the credibility of the project.

Advisers may receive part of their remuneration by way of a success fee paid when the contract is signed (and associated financing is made available). However, caution should be exercised, especially where advisory support is required at the initial stages of project development: the public sector's interests in doing the right project and the adviser's interests in closing a deal, if a large part of its fee is based on successful signing, may not always be aligned. It is generally better to pay advisers when they deliver a predefined work package, covering each identifiable phase of the project's development process. PPPs are not about "doing the deal," but about doing the *right* deal. Finally, the quality and reputation of the public authority's advisers are an important factor for the private sector to consider when assessing whether or not to submit a bid. Good advisers add considerable credibility to a project.

Case Study: Queen Alia Airport Expansion, Amman, Jordan

Project:	Queen Alia International Airport expansion
Description:	25-year contract to upgrade, expand, rehabilitate, operate, and maintain Queen Alia International Airport, Jordan.
Financial close:	December 2007
Capital value:	US$675 million, of which US$370 million is debt and US$305 million is equity
Consortium:	Airport International Group, comprising Abu Dhabi Investment Corporation of Abu Dhabi (40 percent), NOOR of Kuwait (25 percent), J&P Avax of Greece (10 percent), EDGO Investment Holdings of Jordan (10 percent), Joannou & Paraskevaides—J&P Avax subsidiary (10 percent), and Aéroports de Paris Management of France (5 percent)
Lead adviser:	International Finance Corporation
Financiers:	Islamic Development Bank (US$100 million lease); International Finance Corporation (IFC "A loan" of US$70 million; IFC "B loan" of US$160 million provided by Calyon, Europe Arab Bank, and Natixis; IFC "C quasi-equity loan" of US$40 million; US$10 million stand-by facility)

Jordan aims to develop the country's only international airport into a gateway to Africa, Asia, and Europe. Jordan's Queen Alia International Airport (QAIA), located 32 kilometers south of the capital Amman, is an increasingly popular transit point for tourists, business travelers, and international air freight. Passenger traffic has grown 6 percent a year in the last decade, rising to 3.5 million visitors in 2006. According to the Ministry of Transport, the figure is expected to rise to 12.8 million passengers a year by 2030.[3]

In a bid to position the QAIA as a regional financial, trade, and transport hub and meet increasing demand for capacity, the Jordanian government decided to rehabilitate and increase the capacity of the 25-year-old international airport through a concession for a user-fee PPP. This would involve upgrading and operating the existing terminal building and constructing an

---

[3] http://www.mot.gov.jo/en/statistics.

adjacent state-of-the-art terminal building covering 90,000 square meters. However, this project presented several challenges due to legislative changes, high up-front capital costs, and long payback periods that were required for a project of this size. Furthermore, the airport involved an iconic design that had already been chosen and approved. The design had to be brought back into line with the project economics, but with scope for future expansion. Disturbance to operations also had to be minimized during construction. In addition, commercial banks were not willing to provide long-term financing for a project without mitigation of the perceived high political risk in the region.

The Jordanian government appointed the IFC as lead adviser to assist with these challenges.[4] One of its first steps was to commission traffic reports from independent advisers to confirm the volume of air traffic and revenue forecasts and assess the bankability of the design and legal framework. The IFC advisory team then helped the Jordanian government to hold a fair, transparent, and competitive bidding process that attracted most of the leading international and regional airport operators and construction companies. In June 2006 expressions of interest were invited, and 28 responses were received. By October 2006, six consortia were short listed. In May 2007 the Airport International Group was chosen and granted a 25-year contract to upgrade, expand, rehabilitate, operate, and maintain the airport. The new building is expected to be operational in 2012. In exchange for assuming construction, operation, and demand risks, the private partner is entitled to a share of the airport's gross revenue.

The winning consortium combined a strong lead investor, an experienced airport operator, and construction experts from both the region and internationally.

Total project costs of US$675 million are financed through a combination of shareholders' equity, cash from operations, a US$100 million lease provided by the Islamic Development Bank, and a US$280 million financing package provided by the IFC itself, consisting of the following:

- US$70 million, 17-year senior loan
- US$40 million, 18-year subordinated loan with a 15-year grace period to match the cash flows generated during the concession

---

[4] Part of the World Bank Group, the IFC fosters sustainable economic growth in developing countries by financing private sector investment, mobilizing private capital in local and international financial markets, and providing advisory and risk mitigation services to businesses and governments.

- US$10 million stand-by loan to be disbursed in the event that the cash flows generated by existing operations are insufficient to complete the financing of the new terminal during the construction phase
- US$160 million in a 16-year syndication that attracted French banks Calyon and Natixis as well as Europe Arab Bank. It also provided a swap to Airport International Group to minimize the interest rate risk on the transaction.[5]

Key lessons of the project include the following:

- Development finance institutions can play an important role as advisers, financiers, and guarantors in the development and implementation of large, complex PPP projects. Their participation can improve the credibility of a project and provide greater assurance for other providers of long-term finance, investors, and contractors.
- Capacity is important to the effective management and coordination of different advisers.
- Advisers play an important role throughout the process, especially with regard to detailed project preparation and diagnosis *before* launching the bidding phase. This includes realistic demand forecasts, realistic cost estimates, and well-defined project requirements; that is, requirements are not subsequently developed during the bidding phase.
- High-quality project documentation should be prepared in advance of the bid phase.
- Strong management of the bidding phase and a fair, transparent, and competitive bidding process are essential to attracting and retaining interest from high-quality international bidders.
- Effective bid evaluation processes mean that the technical competence, strength, and experience of a well-balanced consortium are as important as the price.
- It is important to integrate project design with project economics and bankability; predesigned iconic designs can present challenges and may not always be bankable.

---

[5] Project Finance International: http://www.pfie.com/.

8.

MANAGING THE INITIAL INTERFACE WITH THE PRIVATE SECTOR

Project selection and preparation are likely to be ineffective if they are not based on a good understanding of how private sector bidders will view the project and what the costs are likely to be. In addition to input from the project advisers, project preparation needs to be informed by continual input from the private sector market.

Can this be done without launching the procurement process itself? Market sounding (or "soft" market testing) is a tool that can provide the public authority with an opportunity to cross-check its thinking about the project with that of private sector specialists, including contractors, lenders, and equity investors, up to the end of the preparation phase (4Ps 2002; United Kingdom, Office of Government Commerce 2005). It provides an essential opportunity for the private sector to deliver feedback on how the packaging and scope of the project could be developed to ensure private sector participation and improve competition. It may also give useful insight into the likely level of market interest, ensuring a better fit between the outcomes required by the public sector and those that the private sector can deliver. Good-quality feedback will come from sophisticated players who have participated in similar schemes in other countries. It is important to identify who these players might be and to encourage them to participate in the process.

While the approach varies depending on the scheme under consideration, the issues commonly covered by market-sounding exercises include the scope of the project, any technical issues affecting the ability of potential bidders to deliver the services, identification of any potential supply-side capacity constraints, expected costs, payment mechanisms, key risks envisaged to be transferred, contractual structures and terms, and proposed timetable for the period from procurement to the commencement of services. Market sounding is not part of the procurement process, and potential participants should be informed that they can take part in the procurement process even if they do not take part in market sounding.

Preparation for Market Sounding

Before launching the market-sounding exercise, it is advisable to prepare a short project briefing note covering matters such as the public sector parties involved, the basic proposals developed to date, the scope of the scheme, availability of land, supporting infrastructure, employment, and any other relevant development opportunities. It is better to be transparent about what is and is not known about the project than to be seen as hiding critical information about it. This briefing note is not intended to sell the project at this stage, as it is still being defined, but it is intended to ensure informed feedback from the market. A list of the specific issues on which the public authority is seeking assistance or feedback from the market should be provided. Clarity about what the authority is trying to achieve is important (backed up by evidence of central government support for the project, if relevant). The list should be worded carefully to encourage the best-quality response. Potential bidders often give vague positive indications of interest in the project just to keep their foot in the door, so the purpose of the questions is to unearth real, specific issues that could derail the project.

Consideration should also be given to the conduct of the market-sounding exercise itself, taking particular account of the need to ensure that the parties responding to the exercise are not given an unfair competitive advantage in any subsequent bidding, that the process is conducted in an open, fair, and transparent way, and that it is properly documented. Although this is not a formal bidding process at this stage, potential bidders will be looking for clues as to how the public authority conducts itself. Thus, while the application of all the procedures governing the interface between the public and the private sectors required in a formal bidding process are not required at this stage and may even constrain efforts to get at the heart of the issues, the market will want to be assured that a solution is not being developed to suit one particular supplier with excessive influence over the public authority. Documenting the proposed process, the market participants approached, and the issues to be addressed and, in some instances, soliciting responses in writing all help to leave a transparent trail of the market-sounding activity. Nevertheless, it is important to avoid misrepresenting the exercise: this process does not seek to receive expressions of interest in the project. Equally, it is not intended to "sound out" a *particular supplier's* ability to meet the requirements; rather it is intended to extrapolate from the discussions a picture of the *market's* likely response. Experienced advisers can make a significant difference in the effectiveness and credibility of the process, but it is important to ensure that they are impartial and do not have a vested interest in a particular outcome.

The market-sounding exercise should not be carried out at too early a stage; in addition to not providing useful input, the public authority will also run the risk of appearing vague and uncertain about its objectives, which will not inspire confidence in its ability to bring the proposal to the market. Equally, it should not be carried out at too late a stage, since the potential for legal difficulties increases as the outline proposal develops into a full procurement. Nevertheless, there may be opportunities at a later stage to harness input from bidders after the proposal becomes a formal procurement opportunity and is advertised, depending on the procurement regulations.

As part of the market-sounding exercise, an up-to-date database should be compiled of likely and appropriate interested private sector contractors, lenders, and investors.

A marketing or open day may be held for interested parties, attended by relevant organizations from the public sector sponsor of the project and by potential private sector bidders. As part of the open day (or as a follow-up), the public sector might obtain further feedback on the scope and content of the project with regard to its attractiveness to the bidding market. This can be done by gathering information through a questionnaire and holding one-on-one meetings. Box 8.1 presents the most important elements of a successful market-sounding exercise.

Before the Launch

Once the project is in a reasonably developed form, but before the procurement phase has been launched, it can be helpful to announce that the project will go to formal advertisement in the near future. This announcement can be made through the release of a brief description of the project, which enables potential bidders to prepare for the procurement process. The project information released at this stage is not extensive (and may even be as short as one page). It may typically include a short description of the nature of the project, scope of work, and possible size of investment, together with the expected timing of the procurement process.

The public sector can often lose sight of the impact and role it has in shaping the market. This means that the project should not be seen in isolation, but as part of a wider program, where relevant. A common mistake is for separate procurement authorities to take similar projects to the market at similar times in an uncoordinated fashion. This overlap may be unavoidable

BOX 8.1

Top 10 Tips for a Successful Market-Sounding Exercise

1. ✓ Make sure that the market-sounding exercise is in line with any relevant procurement rules.
2. ✓ Prepare thoroughly for any interface with the market to get the most out of the exercise and give the best account of the public authority to the world at-large.
3. ✓ Consider market-sounding exercises at an early stage in the project and procurement appraisal process before formulating the procurement plans in detail.
4. ✓ Invest time in preparing the background documentation, be clear about the issues to be discussed with the market (for example, information on proposed risk allocation, compensation, and structure) to ensure that the market has something to respond to, formulate and word questions carefully, avoid jargon.
5. ✓ Be clear about the process to be used to select organizations to help with the market-sounding exercise, such as selecting organizations to interview or inviting organizations to make written submissions.
6. ✓ Consider use of a one-on-one format with the selected organiza-tions; be sensitive to the fact that they might not be at ease with a process that involves simultaneous discussion with two or more potential competitors but reassure all parties that no one is being singled out for special treatment in any subsequent procurement.
7. ✓ Involve more than one individual on the side of the public authority, be consistent about what you say to respondents, and ensure that meetings are documented; make use of market information and feedback, which is the ultimate purpose of the market-sounding exercise.
8. ✗ Do not waste time receiving sales pitches; the point of the exercise is to find out what the market thinks of the proposal so far; equally, avoid being seduced into shaping the project to suit a particular proposal.
9. ✗ Do not restrict the scope of the market sounding in any way; aim for a broad selection of the market, such as inviting both operators

(continued next page)

and construction-related firms and funders, if appropriate; keep an open mind, focusing on outcomes rather than on one particular means of achieving them.

10. ✕ Do not use procurement language such as "bidders" or otherwise give the impression that the market sounding is a procurement opportunity; this stage only seeks to gather information and encourage respondents to be at ease providing critical feedback rather than to feel that they need to be accommodating as potential bidders.

at times (for example, if similar projects are being procured across a whole region), but having an awareness of other projects in the pipeline is helpful to inform the timing of the project launch and the assessment of market interest. The capacity of the local contractors is often one of the main constraints once a program gets under way.

Perception of the Project

The need to engage with the private sector means that the perceptions of the project among potential investors, lenders, and contractors start to be formed at an early stage. Perceptions of the government's commitment to the project, the competence of the public sector project team and its advisers, the timing and manner in which information is released to the market, and how the process is managed are as important as the quality of the information itself. The public authority must conduct itself in such a way as to sell the project's concept to the private sector. These factors are all relevant to transforming a project from a desirable activity in the eyes of government to a business opportunity capable of attracting private sector capital and management in a strong competitive process. See boxes 5.1 and 5.2 in chapter 5 for the major concerns of project lenders, contractors, and investors.

Role of Development Finance Institutions and Donors

Development finance institutions (DFIs) can play an important role in the preparation of a project by acting as a readily accessible sounding board for the project's structure and commercial viability as well as being an important source of long-term funding. They should be involved at an early stage and may be an important component of the market-sounding activity.

As the example of the Queen Alia Airport expansion project shows (see the case study in chapter 7), DFIs can also provide early endorsement of the project by, for example, issuing indicative and conditional terms of finance that bidders may incorporate into their funding structures. While such institutions usually provide only a proportion of the likely funding required, their participation can significantly improve the credibility of the project and provide greater assurance and comfort for the other providers of long-term finance, investors, and contractors, particularly with regard to perceived political risks. Some DFIs also have guarantee instruments that provide a degree of protection for private sector parties with regard to public sector payment and other political risks (Matsukawa and Habeck 2007), as discussed in chapter 5.

Discussions with potential donors may also be important at this stage, giving the public authority an opportunity to explore the willingness and availability of donor funds to support any long-term public sector payment obligations that might be involved (as well as the public authority's costs of project preparation).

Transition to the Procurement Phase

Two issues are of importance during the transition to procurement: a prelaunch check and a competitive process.

Prelaunch Check

Prior to entering the procurement phase, a formal project review is strongly recommended. Such a review helps to ensure that the project is likely to be well received by the market, is affordable, is still expected to deliver value for money, and is supported by the relevant stakeholders. It also helps to ensure that the public sector is prepared for the next phase, reducing the risk of potentially costly failure and embarrassment for the public authority. Table 8.1 provides a checklist of the issues that should be reviewed at this stage.

Importance of Competition

Public authorities should run a competitive process, wherever possible. A well-run competitive process usually delivers a better solution at a lower cost than a process with no competition. It helps to ensure a much firmer foundation for the project by strengthening the acceptance of stakeholders. Insofar as a competitive process requires that the project be designed to elicit genuine interest from multiple bidders, it helps to encourage the development of a market, reducing the dependence on an individual supplier. This may be particularly relevant if the project runs into difficulties and an alternative

Table 8.1 Checklist before Launching the Procurement Phase

Issue	Questions to answer
Clarity of requirements	Are the scope and requirements of the project clear and stable?
Risk allocation	Have the project risks been fully identified and their potential allocation assessed?
Key terms and conditions	Has the draft PPP contract been prepared, reflecting the project requirements and proposed risk allocation?
	Have issues related to external interfaces, agreements, terms, and conditions been identified and assessed?
Indication of commercial interest	Is there evidence of sufficient contractor, lender, and investor market interest to justify launching the project on the proposed terms?
	Has a project marketing strategy and list of prospective bidders been drawn up?
	What are the expected availability and terms of equity and debt finance?
	Have the development finance institutions been approached?
Project information	What plans exist to publicize the launch of the project to potential bidders?
	Has the project team prepared a project information memorandum?
	Have the bidder qualification and bid evaluation criteria been developed?
Affordability	Is the project scope fully affordable?
	Are the user tariffs realistic, and are budgets and approvals in place for any public sector payment (or asset provision) obligations?
Indicative timetable	Is a realistic timetable in place for the procurement phase?
Project team and processes	Is a credible and well-resourced team in place to manage the procurement phase, and is an effective bidding process and evaluation strategy agreed?

(continued next page)

Table 8.1 Checklist before Launching the Procurement Phase *(Continued)*

Issue	Questions to answer
	Are project governance structures and processes in place to ensure timely and effective decision making?
	Are credible and experienced advisers appointed?
	Has the appropriate assessment been carried out to demonstrate that the proposed approach is expected to meet any value-for-money criteria (to the extent required by policy)?
Commitment of stakeholders and users	Have all relevant stakeholders been identified, are they committed to the project, and are arrangements in place for continued communication and consultation?
Legal processes	Have required approvals been identified or obtained (for example, environment, planning)?
	Is there clarity about site and land issues?
	Are all relevant project approvals in place?
	Are appropriate powers confirmed for the public authority to award and enter into long-term contracts, including the commitment of long-term budgetary appropriations?
	Are statutes relating to general contract law and banking law suitable to support PPP project financing?

Source: Authors.

contractor or operator is required later on and thus may prevent the project risks from returning to government. In many countries, competition is a mandatory legal requirement. Above all, given the long-term nature of the contractual relationship under a PPP, this is the only opportunity to use extensive competitive pressure to assure the best deal. If negotiations are with only one bidder, this opportunity is lost.

The requirement for a competitive process means that *a procurement strategy has to be worked out in advance*, which has implications for what information is released to contractors and funders and when and how this is done. This issue is discussed in the next chapter.

9.

MANAGING PROCUREMENT

During the procurement phase, the level of interaction with the private sector increases substantially, but all the important groundwork should already have taken place. During this phase, increasingly detailed information about the project is shared with bidders, and information about bids and bidders is received. The main challenge is to manage the large amounts of information that starts to flow in both directions, while maintaining strong competitive tension and ensuring an auditable trail of activities.

This chapter provides a brief overview of the procurement phase in order to describe its underlying purpose and indicate what might be expected, particularly in relation to engagement with the private sector. This will help to put into perspective the project preparation activities that have been described in preceding chapters. The following discussion is not intended to prescribe any one particular procurement process, nor does it cover this complex phase in any detail. Local laws and regulations, usually designed for procurement across a wide range of activities, not just public-private partnerships (PPPs), will also have a significant bearing on what can and cannot be done.

There is a growing availability of guidance on PPP procurement processes: governments with active PPP programs have often developed detailed procurement rules to encourage good practice and to ensure that processes are aligned with regulations: examples include Australia's Partnerships Victoria, Singapore's Ministry of Finance, South Africa's National Treasury, and the United Kingdom's Her Majesty's Treasury (which, in turn, incorporates European Union procurement legislation), to name a few. Readers should refer to these as more detailed examples of developed practice, while also taking into account their own local legal and administrative practices.[1]

Outcome of the Procurement Phase

The purpose of the procurement phase is usually to develop and conduct a process that accomplishes the following:

- Selects a bid
- Maximizes the benefits of competitive tension between bidders
- Delivers the best bid from the most competent bidder
- Minimizes time and cost
- Stands up to scrutiny from citizens and both the public and private sectors.

These objectives may, however, affect one another: it is possible to select a winning bid quickly and cheaply, but a better one might have been selected through a more careful and thoughtful process. Is the best bid simply the cheapest one, or is it the one that offers the best longer-term value for money (and how is this defined)? It is also possible to select the best bid, but will the process be challenged and face subsequent delays? Will it be efficient? How these issues are balanced is a matter of policy, procurement regulations, and the art of the possible, but in all cases these issues need to be recognized, considered, and an approach agreed upon from the beginning. In summary, there are *processes* and, more fundamentally, *objectives* that are not always easy to reconcile.

Role of Advisers

As mentioned in chapter 7, advisers are central to the procurement phase, particularly in the evaluation of bids, where specialized financial, legal, and technical input may be required, and in the comparison of bid proposals. Well-drafted and comprehensive bidding and submission documents are vital to the smooth running of a project, and the advisers should be closely involved with drafting them. The quality and experience of the public authority's advisers are an important consideration for potential bidders in deciding whether or not to participate. The case of the Inkosi Albert Luthuli Central Hospital (see the case study at the end of this chapter) shows that an experienced set of advisers, well-managed by the public authority, can make a substantial difference to the outcome of the process. The KwaZulu Natal

---

[1] The World Bank and PPIAF's PPP in Infrastructure Resource Center has links to different PPP units that have developed procurement guidance and standardized bidding documents. See www.worldbank.org/pppiresource.

Department of Health (KZN DoH), the procuring authority, was supported by the South African Treasury's PPP unit and by an international team of technical, financial, and legal advisers throughout the procurement process.

Role of Development Finance Institutions

Development finance institutions (DFIs), such as the World Bank Group, are frequently a very important source of long-term finance for PPP projects. However, unlike commercial lenders, many DFIs have their own detailed procurement rules and cannot align themselves with a particular bidder or the procurement practices of a particular country. To reduce the risk of the project not having access to these funding sources, it is important for the public authority to engage DFIs early in the process, if they believe that they are likely to play a significant role, and to ask them to provide a list of common terms and to make this list available to all bidders (see chapter 8). Clearly the DFI will not be able to commit funding until it is satisfied with the quality of the winning bidder.

Bid Stages

The PPP bidding process is usually divided into a series of steps. These steps ensure that increasingly detailed information is provided by both the public and the private sectors and that evaluation takes place to ensure an effective process while minimizing the time and costs required of both parties (see figure 9.1). The other important objective is to elicit comparable bids. Throughout the process, the public authority needs to be mindful of the output requirements and affordability limits of the project.

In the later stages of the procurement process, the public authority is usually more interested in the *quality* than in the quantity of bids. Higher-quality bids (which mean better information on which to base a decision) are likely to be received from a smaller number of well-qualified bidders. With the costs of preparing a bid potentially running into millions of dollars, bidders will put more effort into their submission if a limited number of bidders are involved. Nevertheless, while reducing the number of bidders to a manageable size, the public authority also needs to have enough bidders to ensure strong competition between them. In practice, a target of three to five bidders at the "selection of preferred bidder" stage is quite common, although it is a matter of debate whether an absolute upper or lower (that is, more than two) limit to this figure should be set.

Project Launch

At the initial stage, the objective should be to attract as wide a range of bidders as possible (bidders will often comprise a consortium of parties, as

Figure 9.1 Outline of the Procurement Process

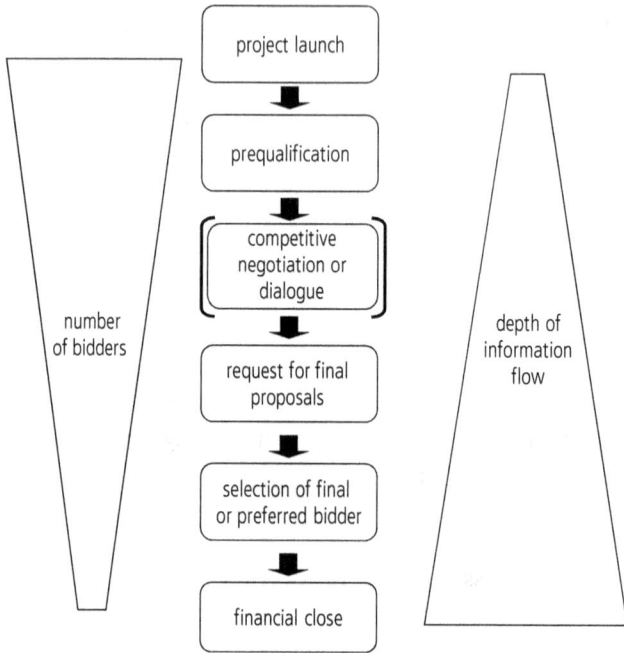

Source: Authors.

described in chapter 4). This process may already have begun during the project preparation phase and through market sounding, even though the procurement phase may not yet have been formally launched (see chapter 6). As one moves though the procurement process, bidders that clearly are not equipped to compete are removed (and there may be a procedure to debrief them at this stage).

The bid process is normally launched by formally releasing details of the project in an official publication that announces public tenders. This helps to ensure transparency, avoid discrimination in the release of information about the project, and attract a wide range of attention. Public sector Web sites and procurement platforms may also be used. Extensive publicity at this stage is required to ensure that the net is cast as widely as possible, both domestically and internationally, so that the best potential bidders are encouraged to participate.[2] It is important to take legal advice when issuing public

---

[2] Many DFIs require publication in the international dgMarket Web site (http://www.dgmarket .com).

tenders to ensure compliance with any applicable procurement laws and therefore reduce the risk of a subsequent challenge to the final bid decision. As circumstances in the market can change significantly over the procurement period, it is generally advisable to ensure that the launch of any tender notice gives the procuring authority some flexibility so that the process does not necessarily have to be restarted from scratch if circumstances change.

The information disclosed at this stage should be sufficient to explain the project and to attract potential bidders, but it is not usually the basis on which bidders will be expected to make firm long-term commitments. Sometimes referred to as a "preliminary information memorandum" or a "prequalification memorandum," this notice should give details of the scheme as envisaged by the public contracting authority and indicate the volume and scope of the services required, expressed in terms of either details of the project or expected monetary values of the project, together with details of the proposed public contracting authority. The information required at this stage is intended to help bidders to determine whether the project is of sufficient interest for them to invest time and resources in investigating the prospect further and to start identifying partners for a possible bidding consortium.

The information should include details of the conditions for prequalification—that is, the information that will be required from bidders to assess their economic and financial standing and technical capacity to prequalify.

The notice may also set out the award criteria for the tender itself (for example, lowest price or most economically advantageous offer) and the relative weighting of the evaluation criteria if relevant, providing assurance, through such transparency, that bids will be evaluated against *clear and consistent* criteria.

The notice normally emphasizes that the project is a PPP scheme and that the bidders will be expected to bear a significant portion of the risks associated with delivery of the project.

Potential bidders may also be invited to obtain a project information memorandum that amplifies the details of the project launch notice and prequalification criteria (see box 9.1).

Bidders may be invited to visit the project site and to meet the public authority (see box 9.2). Good bidders will be very interested in assessing the quality of the public sector team and its advisers before deciding whether to prequalify. It is important to remember that bidders also have their own formal procedures for developing bids, including establishing budgets to cover their own, often extensive, costs of bid development. Usually the bidder's board of directors will have to deliberate and agree to commit resources, which will be at risk and may be significant, before proceeding with bid

BOX 9.1

Project Information Memorandum

Key project information is normally set out in the form of a project information memorandum, which generally covers the following areas: the public contracting authority, project information, and proposed procurement process.

Public Contracting Authority

- Details on the public sector parties involved in the project
- How the public sector team is organized to manage the procurement process
- Details of public sector advisers.

Project Information

- Project rationale and strategic objectives
- Outline of project requirements—scope, services, size, location, potential capital investment, and potential risks expected to be borne by the private sector
- Anticipated payment mechanism (user fees, availability fees, or a combination of these)
- Status of all project approvals, planning consents, and environmental assessments
- Status of public consultation
- Possibly an outline of model designs and design requirements
- Information on enabling works, status, and availability of infrastructure services on which the project may depend
- Potential funding sources (including potential DFI finance).

Proposed Procurement Process

- Stages and anticipated timetable (which might be dictated by legislation or by the DFI's procurement rules)
- Details of any proposed bidders' conference
- Outline of what will be required of bidders at each stage
- Outline of information that will be released at each stage
- Outline of the evaluation at each stage.

BOX 9.2

Bidders' Conference

When procurement begins, the public authority may organize a bidders' conference (also known as bidders' open days). These events are usually organized once the project information memorandum and prequalification questionnaire have been issued to potential bidders (see chapter 8). A bidders' conference allows the public authority to provide potential bidders with more comprehensive information about the project than may be included in the information memorandum and allows potential bidders to seek answers to issues on which they are unclear. Such a conference may also facilitate partnering between different consortium members.

Bidders' conferences may not always be appropriate, especially if the project requirements are relatively straightforward. Instead, some public authorities may prefer to rely on the project information memorandum and to encourage bidders to seek written clarification on any issues of uncertainty. Procurement laws may also prevent bidders' conferences.

The conference involves presentations by the senior public official with overall responsibility for the project and members of the project board or project team. This can be particularly useful if there is any doubt among bidders about the commitment of the public authority to the proposals. Effectively, it is an opportunity for key stakeholders to market the scheme. Using a video presentation to outline key aspects of the project is often preferable to using numerous speakers.

Provided an effective governance system is in place to ensure transparency, individual "one-on-one" sessions may also take place, giving each potential bidder expressing an interest the opportunity to hear more details about the project, either as a separate exercise or in conjunction with formal presentations.

Whatever approach is adopted, it is important to remember that the overriding purpose of the bidders' conference is to "sell" the project and to demonstrate to potential bidders that the public authority has the skills and expertise in place (including the advisory team) to manage the procurement phase in an efficient and transparent way and to deliver on its obligations. It is important for the bidders' conference to be considered early in the procurement process to determine how it fits with other arrangements. Details of the bidders' conference should be included in the project launch notice and the project information memorandum.

preparation. A major factor in the decision to proceed will be the quality of the information provided by the public authority and the extent to which the project has been well prepared for the procurement process, as discussed in the preceding chapters.

Prequalification

The prequalification stage is intended to screen out those bidders that do not meet a threshold of technical and financial capacity to deliver the project (see figure 9.2). This helps to discourage bidders that clearly are unlikely to deliver the project from investing further time and effort in the process, while enabling the public authority to focus on bidders that are more likely to deliver the required project. However, it is also important to ensure that the prequalification criteria and the nature of the projects do not exclude good entrants into the process—this can be a risk with overly mechanical experienced-based qualifying criteria, especially when there is a succession of similar projects.

Having received preliminary details of the project, bidders wishing to participate in the competition may then be instructed to apply for, complete, and

Figure 9.2   Outline of the Prequalification Phase

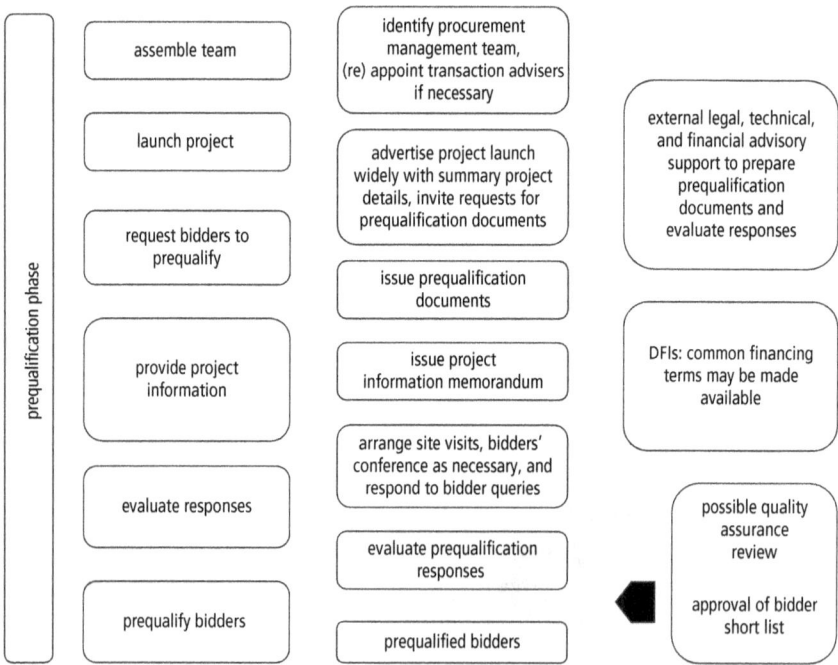

Source: Authors.

return a request for qualification (RfQ) document, sometimes referred to as a prequalification questionnaire (PQQ) or an expression of interest (EoI) document. The public authority then evaluates the RfQ (PQQ or EoI) responses according to the selection criteria set out and produces a short list of qualified bidders. To ensure transparency of the process, an evaluation report may be used that sets out the process followed and how the decision was reached.

At this point, bidders should not be expected to spend significant resources reviewing the project in detail. Information on the quality and capacity of the bidders, not their bids, is what is required at this point in the process. The approach can involve a limited number of objectively measurable pass-fail criteria, as shown in the example given in box 9.3, although care must be taken that, in seeking to use highly objective quantitative criteria (if there is concern about the transparency of more qualitative criteria), the market does not "game" the system and that potentially good-quality bidders are not excluded. The process must, therefore, be continuously and carefully reviewed. A scoring or ranking of criteria may also be used, especially if a target number of short-listed bidders is sought. Policy may

---

BOX 9.3

Summary of RfQ for Public-Private Partnership Projects, Government of India

To prequalify, bidders must pass separate technical and financial capacity tests (see India, Ministry of Finance 2007):

- *Technical experience.* The bidder must, over the past five years, have experience of similar projects equal to the estimated project cost. Eligible projects are defined, and the experience is scored by applying to these numbers a weighting, with the highest weighting going to projects that involve comparable project experience in the sector and the lowest weighting going to projects that involve construction experience but are still in the broader infrastructure sector.
- *Operation and maintenance experience.* The bidder must have a minimum of five years of operational and maintenance experience in the sector in a project of equivalent size.
- *Financial capacity.* The bidder must have a minimum net worth of 25 percent of the project's estimated capital costs.

A limit of up to six bidders may be short listed (there are some exceptions for multiple projects and for certain power projects). The short list must be announced within 50 days after release of the RfQ.

require that consideration be given to encouraging local market partici-pants, and this may be one of the prequalifying factors. The criteria may also involve a wider range of both qualitative and quantitative factors (as found, for example, in the approaches undertaken in Australia, Singapore, South Africa, and the United Kingdom). This approach can provide a much more comprehensive picture of the capability and suitability of bidders and reduce the risk that better bidders will be screened out, which is particularly relevant given the complexity and long-term nature of the eventual partner-ship envisaged. However, this will usually involve more subjective scoring of qualitative issues, which may open the process to the risk of challenge in the absence of strong governance processes or may not be permitted by existing procurement legislation.

Bidders will start to coalesce into consortiums. They must be given time to do so, as the assessment will be on the collective capabilities of the group. Nevertheless, the consortiums should not necessarily be required to con-stitute formally at this stage (although some legal systems require this), as doing so may entail premature expense and commitment by bidders, which could discourage their participation. Encouraging good players to come to the table should be the objective at this initial stage.

In the case study of Inkosi Albert Luthuli Central Hospital (IALCH), described at the end of this chapter, the RfQ documentation set out rules for the procurement process (including the stages, timelines, and format of submissions), a brief description of the project, and guidance on the expected kind of participants. The RfQ also requested verifiable informa-tion on bidders to assess both their qualifications and capacity to deliver the required services. A wide range of 23 South African and international firms responded, and four potential bidders were prequalified.

Procurement laws do not always allow a prequalification phase. Despite the potential benefits that such a phase can offer, some legal systems do not allow this based on a concern that such a process could be misused to pre-vent the participation of certain bidders. However, even in these countries, it can be possible and probably worthwhile to implement a pre-revision phase instead. The contracting authority can review certain documents prior to the formal request for proposals with two goals in mind:

- To discourage bidders who clearly are unlikely to deliver the project from investing further time and effort or encourage those who are likely to do so to strengthen their consortium and become able to deliver the project.
- To provide bidders with feedback regarding the compliance with certain formal requirements, which will reduce the risk of having to disqualify them for not meeting such requirements at a later stage.

Request for Proposals

Unlike the initial phase, with its focus on casting the net as wide as possible, the purpose of the request for proposal (RfP) phase is to encourage the delivery of bids of sufficient *quality* and *comparability* from the prequalified group of good bidders. From these, a bid can be selected that best meets the public authority's criteria, while at the same time ensuring that the process will stand up to scrutiny and accord with the applicable procurement legislation. It is essential that, during this process, strong competitive tension is maintained between bidders, to ensure that a sufficient number of good bidders stay in the race. A single-bidder situation, and therefore the loss of competitive tension to drive a good deal for the procuring authority, must be avoided wherever possible and is usually the result of a poorly prepared project or a badly run bidding process.

The important factors at this stage are, therefore, the quality and clarity of the bid documents (including the instruction to bidders), the output specifications, the proposed contract documents, and the efficiency with which the process is run. At this stage, good advisers can make a significant difference. The clearer the bid documents and the process are, the clearer the responses will be, the quicker and easier it will be to measure and compare bids, and the greater the chance will be of retaining good bidders in the race. Having an efficient process helps to reduce the costs of submitting and evaluating the bids, which can be significant.

This stage may involve a single submission of bids from prequalified bidders within an established timetable. This may be preceded by a process in which prequalified bidders seek clarifications about the bid requirements and even a process of refining the contract documentation based on comments from bidders. Once bids have been submitted, there may be a mechanism to clarify details of the submissions, but without further changes to the scope of the project or the bids submitted.

Other processes can involve a form of structured dialogue between the bidders and the public authority *before* arriving at the final submission of a smaller number of comparable bids from which to select a winning bid. This approach is generally appropriate for complex projects, as it enables the public authority's requirements to be fine-tuned to the capabilities in the market and provides a much greater level of scrutiny on the capability of the bidders and their proposed solutions. Such a dialogue may only need to focus on a limited number of key project issues. However, it requires greater sophistication on the part of the public authority in managing the dialogue in a transparent, competitive, and efficient way, as well as mechanisms to ensure that one bidder's solution is not revealed to other bidders. A form of such a process is used, for example, in the European Union, where it is known as "competitive dialogue." In Victoria, Australia, the "interactive" bidding process is used for a broadly similar purpose. The use of such approaches also depends on what the procurement regulations (or the rules of the concerned DFI, if relevant) will permit.

At the end of the single-tender submission or dialogue/interactive phase, selection of a final or preferred bidder takes place following a predetermined evaluation process (see figure 9.3). This evaluation may be as simple as a single parameter, such as the lowest overall price, smallest share of revenue, or lowest subsidy, or it may involve a more sophisticated balance of quality as well as price—sometimes referred to as the "most economically advantageous tender." (Bidders may even be invited to propose alternative solutions, known as "variant bids," alongside their conforming bids, that may present an alternative and improved approach.)

Evaluation of both price and other qualities is likely to lead to a better long-term choice of bid and bidder than a decision based on a single parameter, as it enables a greater depth of analysis of the bidder's capability, understanding of the project requirements, and proposed technical and financial

Figure 9.3   Outline of the Request-for-Proposals and Financial Close Phase

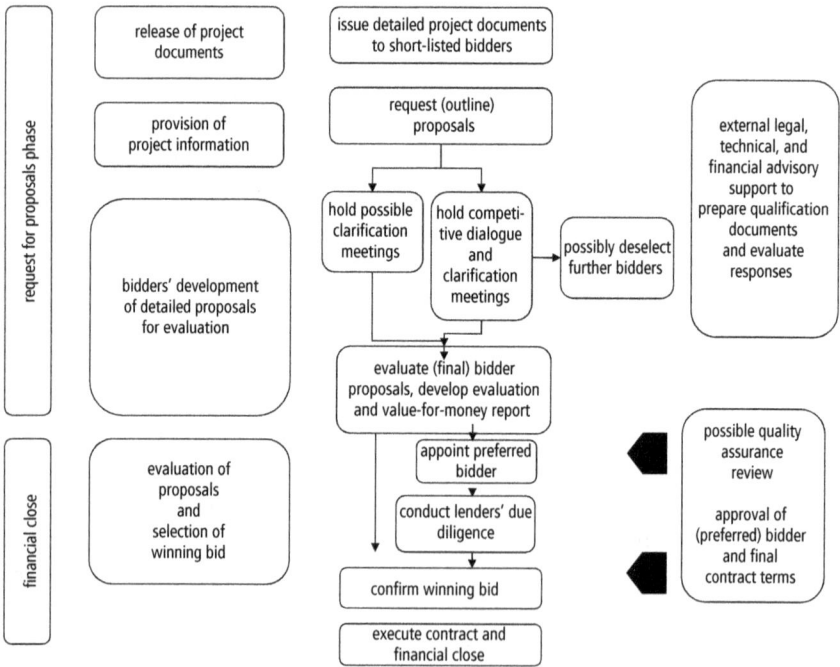

Source: Authors.

solution. The cheapest bid does not necessarily provide the best value for money. However, such an approach can present challenges to ensuring objectivity and transparency of the process as well as understanding the additional complexity, time, and cost involved. Methods have been developed involving a predetermined and detailed scoring mechanism with carefully managed evaluation teams, recorded decision making for audit purposes, and even the use of an independent review entity. Nevertheless, existing procurement laws and rules, distrust of public officials, lack of capacity, and the risk of challenges from losing bidders can be significant obstacles in emerging PPP markets, and the benefits of a more sophisticated bid evaluation process will need to be weighed against what is possible.

Information Provided to Bidders

The information provided to bidders during this phase is much more detailed. It includes the full PPP pro forma contract documents containing the output specifications, payment mechanisms, risk allocation, model designs, and plans, together with detailed background information that may be required for bidders and lenders to carry out their detailed due diligence of the project. The public authority may also set out its ideas on the financial structure for the project, but generally will allow the bidding consortiums to determine the structure. Details of the process, evaluation criteria, and timetable are also provided.

It is important for the timetable for submission of proposals to be realistic. They need to assemble their own bid teams and appoint advisers; carry out their own due diligence of the project information; firm up detailed arrangements between consortium members and often numerous subcontractors (which, in turn, need to be assessed for their capability, as discussed in chapter 5); obtain necessary management and other approvals; develop detailed financial models; negotiate pricing arrangements and terms, which need to work across the various subcontractors; and, in some cases, seek firm commitments of long-term funding from lenders. A common private sector complaint is that the timetable for this is often too short. An excessively ambitious timetable may leave substantial problems for later, when issues that were not resolved during the competitive process are opened up again by the selected bidder in a noncompetitive environment. Equally, the public authority must be organized to respond quickly to bidder requests and keep the momentum of the project going.

A project data room may also be established where detailed project documents can be reviewed. Unless there are strong value-for-money reasons to do otherwise, the public authority should not warrant the accuracy or otherwise of the project information provided. Further project site visits may also be organized for bidders as a useful way to inform them of the project.

As the IALCH case study shows, RfP documents for that project were issued to four prequalified bidders. These documents contained detailed background information on the project and the public authority's service requirements. They also contained information on project assets, the procurement process, timetable and bidder requirements, bidder warranties, grounds for disqualification, requirements for variant bids, arrangements with third parties, and associated risk allocation with respect to the availability of utilities. A data room with project information was provided with very limited warranties by the public authority of the information provided. The RfP also contained the pro forma PPP agreement and set out the proposed payment mechanism, expressed as a single unitary payment with its associated indexation and penalty deductions.

Information Required from Bidders

The invitation sets out what information is required from bidders on their bids and when and how it needs to be submitted. To ensure comparability, especially where information on legal, financial, and technical criteria is required, a series of common headings and financial and economic assumptions may be provided. This enables bidders to submit detailed information in a common and therefore comparable format on the relevant aspects of their bids, a part of which may be in the form of a financial model.

Preferred Bidder and Financial Close

Following any clarification of bids submitted at the end of the RfP or dialogue phase, the public authority then selects a bid based on the evaluation criteria previously provided to the bidders. Evaluation teams, assisted by the transaction advisers, may be established to examine different aspects of the bid. Their findings are typically reported to the project board, which is responsible for choosing the winning bid. A clear audit trail, recording the decision-making processes, should be maintained. For instance, in the IALCH case, the evaluation of each bid was split into four broad criteria: technical, legal, financial, and black economic empowerment (BEE). Each category was further divided into a larger number of subcategories. Technical evaluation teams (TETs) then analyzed the technical, legal, financial, BEE, and price streams as well as the bidder's understanding of the project requirements. Evaluation comprised a balance of weighted scoring and notes. The TETs passed their reports and score sheets to an evaluation coordination committee in charge of selecting the preferred bidder based on the reports and score sheets provided.

It is not unusual for this stage to be followed by a period in which the potential lenders finalize their detailed due diligence of the project before long-term financial commitments are made and financial close of the project is achieved.[3] In this case, a "preferred bidder" may be selected, to be confirmed once committed financing proposals have been submitted and the final terms of the contract have been established.[4] There are risks that changes may be required of the project as a result of the lenders' due diligence on the preferred bid and after competitive tension has been lost. In some cases, this risk may be transferred to the contractor, if the terms of the concession are not negotiable, by requiring bidders to reach financial close within a certain period, which entails the immediate termination of the contract if such obligation is not met. Or bidders may be asked to provide a financial bond (a "bid bond") to the public authority, which may be called for payment if a selected bidder fails to complete the financing and commit contractually within a specified time period. The decision to use bid bonds will depend on the circumstances. Bid bonds may constitute a disincentive to less committed bidders with poorly developed finance plans. However, the complexity of the project may require bidders to invest heavily in the process in any case, so demonstrating their commitment. As an additional cost, the requirement for a bid bond may then act as a disincentive for serious bidders, especially if there is concern about attracting enough bidders to the process. The transaction advisers can help the public authority to determine the best approach. In any case, during periods of stress in the international financial markets, it is not unusual to see a process that confirms financial commitments at this stage rather than earlier.

Prior to contract signing, a formal approval process often takes place within the public authority. This confirms whether the final terms of the deal deliver the requirements on an acceptable basis, whether the procurement process has been carried out in accordance with procurement procedures, and whether decisions have been recorded correctly with the appropriate audit trail. If a standardized form of contract is used, there may be a check to review and assess the justification for the departure from any standard terms. There may also be a further value-for-money assessment, which may focus, in particular, on the quality of the competitive process. These checks form part of the quality control process at the final business case stage and are critical because, once the project agreement has been signed, any subsequent changes can be very costly.

---

[3] "Financial close" means that both the contract and the financing documentation have been signed and that all of the conditions required by these documents have been met.

[4] In some cases, a separate competition between lenders may be held after selection of the preferred bidder.

Case Study: Inkosi Albert Luthuli Central Hospital, South Africa

Project:	Inkosi Albert Luthuli Central Hospital
Description:	Upgrading and management of facilities and information technology of an 846-bed state-of-the art referral hospital in Durban, South Africa, one of the largest and most advanced facilities of its kind in Africa. The project involved a 15-year availability-based payment contract.
Financial close:	February 2002
Capital value:	R$746 million (2001) of which R$60 million was financed by equity and R$326 million was financed by long-term debt. There was a R$360 million capital contribution from KwaZulu Natal Department of Health.
Consortium:	Impilo Consortium, comprising Siemens Medical Solutions (31 percent), Vulindlela Holdings (26 percent), AME Austria (20 percent), Drake & Scull (9 percent), Mbekani (7 percent), and Omame (7 percent).
Financiers:	Rand Merchant Bank

The Inkosi Albert Luthuli Central Hospital is a central tertiary care, referral hospital, located in Mayville, Durban, where a private partner, the Impilo Consortium, provides all of the nonclinical services under a 15-year public-private partnership agreement with the KwaZulu Natal Department of Health (KZN DoH). The general opinion of stakeholders over the past seven years of operation is that this PPP is helping to deliver a level of service that could not have been achieved by the public sector alone.

The hospital provides highly specialized services for the entire population of KwaZulu Natal and half of the Eastern Cape Province. The hospital is fully computerized and works on paperless principles. It uses leading-edge medical equipment, from magnetic resonance imaging machines to surgical instruments, and was the first hospital in South Africa to enter into a PPP for the delivery of all its nonclinical services. It was also the first South African PPP to be conducted according to South Africa's Treasury Regulation 16.

After a process of initial investigation of PPPs internationally, KZN DoH appointed transaction advisers for the project in 2000. A formal feasibility study and options analysis of the project was conducted, the result of which concluded that entering into a PPP under which the private sector would deliver all nonclinical services would bring value for money and significant risk transfer.

After a detailed RfQ and RfP process, the Impilo Consortium was selected, and the contract documents were signed in December 2001, with financial closure in February 2002. The time frame—just over one year from prequalification to contract signature—was relatively short for a PPP of the size and complexity of IALCH. This was, in part, because all parties were willing to commit time and resources to the negotiation process and to resolve the issues that arose.

An annual unitary payment of R$304.9 million (2001), linked to the consumer price index, is paid in monthly installments. Service levels were set at state-of-the-art levels, with, for example, five-year replacement schedules for medical equipment and three-year replacement schedules for information and management technology.

With regard to the roles and responsibilities of the private partners, Siemens provides all of the automated medical equipment and services, Drake & Scull is responsible for the facilities management, laundry, and catering, while AME Austria is in charge of information technology. The consortium will provide the hospital with services and equipment for the next 15 years, after which the equipment will be handed over to the KZN DoH, if the contract is not renewed.

The Procurement Process

In November 2000, KZN DoH, the procuring authority, launched the initial request for qualifications. This followed an extensive period of preparation, which included a market sounding, the development of a draft PPP agreement, and the associated output-based specifications and payment mechanism. The KZN DoH and transaction advisers had conducted a detailed room-by-room list of equipment, developed an information technology plan for the hospital, analyzed the human resource requirements and costs, and conducted a facilities life-cycle costing exercise. From this, costs for the life of the project were derived, especially for the initial and replacement capital costs of equipment and information technology, the clinical human resource costs, and the consumables and facility capital and operating costs. This allowed a detailed output specification to be developed.

The RfQ documentation set out the rules for the procurement process: stages, timelines, submission format, a brief description of the project, guidance on the expected kind of participants, and requested verifiable information on bidders for evaluation to assess both their qualifications and capacity to deliver the required services.

A wide range of 23 domestic and international firms responded, and four prequalified potential bidders were selected by December 2000. Each prequalified bidder was asked to post a bid bond based on a value equivalent to the costs of restarting the bid process (from the RfQ stage onward) to ensure their seriousness of intent.

Following approval of the South African Treasury, RfP documents were then issued to the prequalified bidders in January 2001. This was followed by a process of dialogue involving both a bidders' conference and one-on-one meetings with prequalified bidders, during which several comments were raised and incorporated into the documentation by means of bidder notes. These documents contained detailed background information on the project and the public authority's service requirements. It also contained information on project assets, the procurement process, timetable and bidder requirements, bidder warranties, grounds for disqualification, requirements for variant bids, arrangements with third parties, and associated risk allocation with respect to the availability of utilities. A data room with project information was provided with minimal warranty by the public authority of the information provided. The RfP also contained the pro forma PPP agreement and set out the proposed payment mechanism, expressed as a single unitary payment with its associated indexation and penalty deductions. One-on-one meetings enabled bidders to request clarity on the RfP and ask confidential questions before the submission of proposals. Bidders were asked to respond with detailed components to the service-level agreements and to provide detailed financial models to allow the public authority to interrogate the bids and test them for their financial robustness. Consortia changes were allowed during bidding, subject to the consent of the public authority and subject to the new members satisfying the RfQ evaluation criteria. Variant bids were permitted, and these were treated as separate from the compliant bids.

The bidders had nine weeks to submit their bids. Although this time period was very short, no serious issues arose, although the bidders were not able to do as full a due diligence on the existing hospital facility as they might have wished.

The evaluation of each bid was split into four broad categories: technical, legal, financial, and black economic empowerment, with each category weighted as follows: (a) technical (70 percent), of which facilities management (20 percent), information and technology management (25 percent), and equipment (25 percent); (b) legal (10 percent); (c) financial and price (10 percent); and (d) BEE (10 percent). It is worth noting that price had a weight of only 10 percent in the total for the evaluation.

Each category was further divided into a larger number of subcategories, such as quality of safety plans, integration with existing services, and percentage of debt to be covered in the event of private party default. There was also a separate evaluation of the overall integration of the bid in delivering value for money.

Bids were checked for completeness and compliance before detailed analysis was undertaken. Clarification of the submitted proposals was also allowed during evaluation, but changes to bidders' proposals were not permitted. Separate technical evaluation teams analyzed the service delivery, legal, financial and price, and BEE streams as well as the bidders' understanding of the project requirements. Evaluation comprised a balance of weighted scoring and notes. The TETs passed their reports and score sheets to an evaluation coordination committee, which oversaw their work and evaluated the overall integrated solution for the project. A single recommendation on process outcome was prepared for a project evaluation committee, which also selected the preferred and the reserve bidders, based on the score sheets from the TETs.

The evaluation coordination committee drew experts from the procuring authority, the national PPP unit, the United Kingdom's National Health Service, and Partnerships UK.

A final negotiation phase then took place with the preferred bidder to finalize detailed project and funding agreements. This culminated in a PPP agreement signed in December 2001 and the commitment of funding in February 2002.

Throughout the process, the public authority was supported by a team of advisers comprising PricewaterhouseCoopers, a law firm (White & Case), chartered accountants (Gobodo), a United Kingdom–based hospital project consultancy (Hiltron), and an engineering firm (Saicog). The South African Treasury's PPP unit worked closely with the procuring authority throughout the process.

Results Achieved So Far
The IALCH commissioning commenced in March 2002 and was completed over the next 12 months. The hospital received its first patients on June 28, 2002, and stakeholders to the agreement are overwhelmingly positive in their view of what the PPP has managed to deliver since then. They firmly believe that the public sector would not have been able to deliver services on the same scale. There have been very few penalty deductions, and service levels have been good. A senior manager at IALCH says that she "would not trade the PPP for anything." A member of the hospital board, who is a community representative, says that the hospital had to overcome some

initial resistance, but now is seen in a very positive light, with patients being satisfied with the service provided. He believes that the partnership between the private partner and KZN DoH is strong and built on mutual trust. Open discussion between all of the players, including the community, has been indispensable in creating this trust.

The very high technical specification for the hospital has raised issues of affordability, and, because the Department of Health has not fully rationalized services elsewhere to consolidate them into IALCH, occupancy rates have been lower than anticipated. Commissioning also has been slower than anticipated due to staff shortages in the public sector.

The PPP is, however, delivering its required objectives. To ensure that it delivers the best possible value for money, it will be important to strengthen public sector management as a whole as well as management of the contract.

Lessons Learned

It is important to be prepared. The project documentation, evaluation, and governance requirements should not be underestimated, and it is vital to have these requirements in place before they are required.

It is also important to encourage bids from credible bidders, not just any bidders. Equally, the public authority and its advisers need to be perceived as credible and committed, and the prequalification process needs to be capable of selecting potential bidders that are likely to be able to deliver.

A clearly agreed evaluation process with separate evaluation teams, a governance structure, and internal and external scrutiny enables the bid evaluation process to take place in a transparent way. It also allows both quantitative and qualitative aspects of the bids to be evaluated, especially with projects that involve complex technical solutions.

Although not PPP specific, it is important to ensure that the service requirements are affordable and that full use of the services purchased is not hampered by deficiencies in the wider public service.

More specific lessons were also learned, such as the following.[5]

Project Inception: Use of Advisers

- Learn from international expertise, especially if none is available locally.
- Ensure that the transaction adviser consortium is multidisciplinary and contains experts in *all* fields necessary to the project; evaluation and appointment of advisers are a critical issue.

---

[5] Information based on a study commissioned by the South African Treasury's PPP unit.

- Involve international experts in the process if local expertise is scarce; this may make the process more complex, but adds significant value if managed correctly.
- Ensure that members of the transaction adviser consortium are as familiar as possible with the project and its environment, especially where there are international members.

Project Financing and Management

- Think creatively about how to finance the deal.
- Make provision for reexamining output specifications once the contract has been running for a while, as feasibility studies are not an exact science.

Procurement

- Ensure that the scope and requirements of the project are clearly defined.
- Set tight, but achievable, deadlines.
- Ensure that people in the highest positions from both the private and public partner are involved and committed.
- Set up a central PPP unit to facilitate and guide the overall process.
- Involve committed decision makers from both sides and avoid the need to refer continuously upward for approval.

10.

AFTER SIGNING

A public-private partnership (PPP) project should be considered a success not simply at financial close, but when construction is complete and a satisfactory level of the services contracted for is being delivered on a sustainable basis.

Managing Contracts

Managing contracts is a process that takes place throughout the life of the PPP.[1] Furthermore, contract management is not just a "legal exercise." Rather, it seeks to ensure the proper delivery of public services and continued delivery of value for money, which will be determined by all components of the project, including the design, construction, and operation of the facility. In order to facilitate success, human and financial resources and the necessary regulatory or contract management arrangements need to be established for the construction phase, the commissioning stage, and the operational stage; the planning for this should take place during the project preparation phase, that is, well ahead of contract signature. If a regulatory framework is already in place when the project is developed, it is also important to think about the necessary resources (human and others) that are available to have a smooth interface with the regulator, if relevant, to the project.

For user-fee PPPs, a regulatory framework may be required to ensure that the terms of the contract are maintained and the interests of users are protected. The framework may also regulate how user charges are adjusted in accordance with a mechanism set out in the concession agreement (typically

---

[1] Nevertheless, it is often the case, even in more mature PPP programs, that the culture of making the deal, rather than managing the contract, sometimes prevails (United Kingdom, National Audit Office 2009).

aiming to maintain an alignment between the project's rate of return and its cost of capital over the medium term).

For an availability-based PPP project, management of the contract may require even greater involvement of the public authority, as it assumes direct responsibility for the periodic payment of performance-based payments in accordance with the terms of the contract. In these cases, the public authority has the responsibility to manage the contract in accordance with the agreed terms, not a separate independent regulator. The team supervising the contract will be responsible for implementing the payment mechanism set out within the contract, which determines, in great detail, how the availability charge is calculated as well as the provisions for dealing with any changes.

The importance of regulation and contract management should not be underestimated. A study of user-fee PPPs in Latin America in the 1990s highlights many of the problems that can emerge during this phase (Guasch 2004): operators that fail to comply with contractual obligations (such as further investment) and high incidences of contract renegotiation and even abandonment of concessions by the private party. Typical problems include poorly drafted contracts, bidding processes that encourage "low ball" or very aggressive tendering, underresourced regulatory bodies (often at a disadvantage to the private operators with respect to the necessary information), and difficulties of enforcement. The seeds for success or failure of the contract management phase are sown by many of the actions or inactions during the project preparation and procurement phases referred to in previous chapters. Research has suggested that the stability and predictability of both the legal regime and, where relevant, the funding for the regulator itself as well as the regulator's decision-making autonomy are the key elements for effective regulation (see, for example, Sirtaine and others 2005). *All* of these elements, not just some—that is, legal clarity, adequate financial capacity, and decision-making autonomy—need to be in place. For availability-based PPPs, similar principles apply to the need for a properly resourced and appropriately empowered contract management team.

The PPP contract will require the private partner to provide regular information on the performance of the project. The contract will give the public sector the right to inspect and audit whenever necessary and often oblige the private party to carry out and submit periodic user surveys. The contract should therefore set out clearly the data requirements for post-signature monitoring by the regulator or other monitoring entity.[2] An "independent

---

[2] See Pardina and Rapti (2007) and Shugart and Alexander (2009) on good practices for establishing a sound regulatory accounting.

engineer" and other specialists may be appointed to provide an independent opinion as to the progress and achievement of prespecified objectives and to inspect the development of the project on a regular schedule, reporting to the public authority on progress, safety, and environmental issues. The independent engineer serves as the "eyes and ears" of the authority, having the necessary technical capacity to supervise the performance of the project in special technical matters in all phases, from construction to operation and delivery of services (including assisting the public authority during any relevant tariff review periods). Both the public authority and the lenders have a vested interest in ensuring that both investment and operation are managed properly, and it is the incentive of having capital at risk that ultimately drives the private party to perform.

The Sofia Water System concession case study at the end of this chapter illustrates the importance of having an independent body to regulate tariffs and monitor performance of the project. It is also a good example of how user-fee PPPs, which involve direct interface with consumers, can present challenges for contract monitoring, especially in politically sensitive sectors such as water distribution. When the project agreement was drafted, there was no national water regulator in Bulgaria. However, the Municipality of Sofia recognized that it was important in the case of this user-fee PPP to establish a dedicated unit of specialists to monitor the concession's performance and control tariffs. The concession agreement provided for this.

Availability-based PPPs will usually involve a mechanism (often called a "payment mechanism") under which the public authority will make long-term, regular payments to the private sector partner against the provision of services as set out in the contract. The performance-based payments will normally be made on a monthly or quarterly basis. This means that detailed contract performance data need to be fed back to the public authority on a regular basis to help it to determine both the performance-based payments and any deductions that may need to be applied if the service is unavailable or below the contracted quality. The public authority responsible for managing the contract will have rights to check the availability and management performance systems through planned and random spot checks. User surveys and monitoring groups made up of relevant stakeholders can also be used to inform the assessment of contract performance. The challenge of ensuring an effective, efficient, and transparent process should not be underestimated. *This challenge should be considered carefully in the initial decision to use such a form of PPP, in the design of the contract, and in judgments about its acceptability to the market.*

It should be expected that changes to the project will occur and that these will need to be managed. A well-structured PPP contract would set out the provisions for handling changes in contract terms and managing failure of the contractor and other adverse events (see box 10.1). Examples of change may include refinancing of the project (typically after construction, when the lower risk profile may enable the project to attract better terms for finance), market testing or benchmarking (which may be used to adjust the cost of some elements of the service provision periodically), and other tariff changes or changes in elements of the service or scope. Or it might involve managing the division of future income for services shared between the public and private parties. It could also refer to changes in the laws and in the structure

---

BOX 10.1

Tips on Managing Contracts

- Consider establishing an experienced contract management support group in the PPP unit, agency, or inter-institutional commission in charge of the PPP program to help contract managers to handle less frequent but more complex issues, such as changes in scope or refinancing.
- Consider reengaging the advisers employed during the procurement phase to support the contract implementation phase (and include provision for this in the procurement of advisers and their terms of engagement and necessary budgets).
- Develop a contract administration manual to bring together information on the terms of the contract and the processes and procedures for managing it, including responsibilities and timelines. Consider involving the private partner in this, for example, in the handling of any interface processes.
- Maintain key contract documents on a shared basis with the private party to avoid misunderstandings. In addition to the project agreement and performance measurement schedules, this may include the financial model.
- Consider producing user guides to assist service users who are involved in contract monitoring, including specific guidelines for involving and consulting groups of customers during the design, bidding, and project implementation process.
- If a payment mechanism or tariff review procedure is involved, carry out a trial run of the mechanism before the contract is signed to test out the system in "real life" scenarios.

(continued next page)

- Remember that this is about ensuring performance throughout the operational period, not just a bureaucratic exercise in "managing the contract"—a good partnership will allow for some flexibility to enable sensible approaches to be taken to problems and unforeseen issues.
- Consider holding planning and training days involving both the public authority and the private party to encourage better understanding between them.
- Ensure continuing review and monitoring of risks, using the risk register and risk matrix developed during the project preparation phase, even though risk allocation would normally be set in the contract, as the public partner will have to manage retained or shared risks.
- Have a detailed communications strategy for dealing with the private party, service users, and stakeholders and review and update it regularly; good communication is a key to ensuring that issues can be resolved.

of the markets. A well-prepared contract will have mechanisms for dealing with such changes. The key message is that there is still a need for active management by the public authority, and it is therefore important to plan for managing changes and other activities anticipated *within* the terms of the contract (as opposed to managing the changes *to* the contract, which may result from not having prepared and negotiated contracts properly in the first place). During the project preparation phase, *consideration must be given to establishing a proper budget for the public authority's cost of monitoring the long-term contract and, where relevant, identifying the contract manager and the team and ensuring that they are trained and familiar with the terms of the contract.* For availability-based PPPs in particular, the contracting authority will subsequently be closely involved in managing the contract. However, those involved with the procurement phase may often move to other positions before the contract management phase begins. Therefore, in the final stages of the procurement phase, it is strongly advisable to involve those who will later be managing the contract, so that they become familiar with the project and the PPP contract terms. Involving contract managers in the procurement phase can also help to ensure that operational issues are better reflected in the terms of the contract. Establishing a source of specialist support for contract managers in a central PPP unit is particularly helpful for dealing with complex issues, such as refinancing, that may only occur from time to time in a contract's life. The specialist unit might also develop guidance on contract management issues. The U.K. Treasury's operational task force and the South African Treasury's contract management support team are examples of this, as is the guidance developed by Partnerships Victoria (Partnerships Victoria 2003a; South Africa, National Treasury 2004c; United Kingdom, Her Majesty's Treasury 2007).

Evaluating PPP Projects and Programs

Evaluation of PPP projects is important, not only as a means to ensure that policy objectives are being met (for example, value for money) and to check if the expected benefits are being realized but also as a vital source of information providing lessons that can be fed back into further development of the PPP policies and processes. Evaluation can improve, for example, the approach to the market or the contractual structures and risk allocation.

Evaluation, or the carrying out of such "performance audits," requires the establishment of methods and specialist capacity within government to carry out this process: national audit bodies are often tasked with this activity. To maintain independence, these bodies usually carry out their evaluation after contract signature, although in some countries—the Audit Court, the Tribunal de Contas da União, in Brazil, for example—they may be part of the project approval process. When to evaluate is usually a balance of getting timely information quickly to inform current processes and obtaining useful data after a meaningful period of performance. An evaluation 12–18 months after the commencement of operations will provide information on the bidding process, the delivery of the project asset, and initial performance. Subsequent evaluations will provide better information on operational performance issues. The detailed processes are beyond the scope of this guide, but examples of guidance on how this may be done are available: the United Kingdom's National Audit Office (2006) uses a matrix of six indicators for six key stages of the project life. India's Comptroller and Auditor General also has established guidelines. Making performance audit reports publicly available also helps to ensure greater transparency by informing a wider audience of policy makers and citizens on the issues. This leads to more informed debate on the appropriate use of PPPs.

PPP units themselves also have a role to play in continually examining the process and linking the lessons learned with continuous improvement of how PPP projects are procured and managed. Markets should be expected to change, and successful implementation and management of PPP programs need both to shape and to respond to such changes.

Case Study: Sofia Water, Bulgaria

Project: Sofia Water System concession
Description: 25-year concession agreement to finance, develop, operate, and maintain the Municipality of Sofia's water and wastewater infrastructure; the concession agreement can be extended for 10 years in accordance with the Municipal Property Act
Financial close: October 2000
Capital value: US$398.55 million, of which US$82.95 million (21 percent) is equity and US$315.60 million (79 percent) is debt
Consortium: Sofiyska Voda, comprising United Utilities/International Water (56.25 percent), Municipality of Sofia (25 percent), and European Bank for Reconstruction and Development (18.75 percent)
Financiers: European Bank for Reconstruction and Development

Before 2000 the Municipality of Sofia, through its utility company Vodosnabdajavne I Kanalizatsia EAD, was responsible for operating and maintaining the city's water supply and sanitation networks, which serve an area covering about 1.3 million people. However, Sofia's water and wastewater system, mostly completed in the 1930s, was deteriorating rapidly because of the lack of adequate maintenance and capital investment, and the number of emergency leakages gradually increased to unacceptable levels. For this reason, the municipality approached the European Bank for Reconstruction and Development (EBRD) in 1996 and asked for support in preparing and executing a competitive bidding process to select an international concessionaire to rehabilitate, upgrade, operate, and maintain Sofia's water and wastewater infrastructure.

The EBRD assisted the municipality in defining parameters for private sector participation and mobilizing independent advisers who worked with the municipality to prepare the project and select a concessionaire through open and competitive international bidding. The bidding followed a three-stage process: (a) prequalification, (b) preparation of bids, and (c) clarifications with the preferred bidder. The initial prequalification round, which included identification of bids and a background check on the potential bidders' capacity to manage the contract, commenced in April 1999 and was completed in May 1999. It was followed by a detailed round of bidding (a period between June to October 1999) and then a final review prior to award of the concession. Final submissions consisted of two envelopes: one envelope containing the lowest combined tariff from the bidders and a second envelope containing an irrevocable commitment to a minimum capital investment of US$150 million and detailed technical strategies in areas such as asset management and customer care. Throughout the bidding process, the EBRD played an important role as guarantor of the transparency of the process. The bidding process generated considerable interest from the leading international water companies, with eight consortia seeking prequalification, and four consortia (later reduced to three by merger) invited to prepare detailed bids. All three final consortia—International Water, Suez Lyonnaise des Eaux, and Vivendi/Marubeni/Berliner Wasser Betriebe—submitted bids in full compliance with the tender rules, a mark of the success of the process. In September 1999 Sofia Water (Sofiyska Voda) was selected as the preferred bidder on the basis of its tariff proposal, and in October 2000 the concession contract was signed.

A factor of significant impact during the tender process was the relatively short timetable of the bid process, which resulted in several issues that could not be resolved satisfactorily prior to, and during, the bid process. As a result, the pragmatic way forward was to establish a series of *conditions precedent* in the concession contract, which both the municipality and the private operator had to fulfill. As a result, although the contract with Sofia Water was signed in December 1999, it did not become effective (that is, reach "financial close"[3]) until the first quarter of 2000.

The municipality took a 25 percent stake in the winning consortium, comprising International Water and United Utilities. EBRD provided a loan to support Sofia Water's capital expenditure program for the first five years of the concession, including start-up costs. Initial investments concentrated on rehabilitation of the water and sewerage networks to reduce leakage and infiltration, actions to ensure reliable supply, and improvements in billing and financial management.[4]

The 25-year concession contract gave Sofia Water the responsibility for all financing and activities associated with maintaining and upgrading the infrastructure of Sofia for the treatment and distribution of freshwater and the collection of sewerage, while keeping ownership of the assets themselves

---

[3] Financial close in the concession contract is defined as the moment in which both parties in the contract have fulfilled all conditions precedent to the satisfaction of the other party.

[4] http://www.ebrd.com/new/pressrel/2000/112dec15x.htm.

in the hands of the municipality. Ownership of new infrastructure assets, constructed by Sofia Water, was also vested in the Municipality of Sophia. Sofia Water was given the right to use those assets, both existing and future, in accordance with its rights and obligations under the concession contract. The concession contains provisions dealing with service standards, tariff adjustments, and dispute resolution. Sofia Water charges an agreed tariff to consumers, and the income from this is used to recoup the investment, cover operating costs, and generate a profit for the concessionaire. There is no availability-based payment.

Service Standards

Under the concession agreement, the concessionaire is required to meet an extensive list of service standards or targets, such as drinking water quality, minimum pressure, and reduction of leakage, many of which were considerably more rigorous than the levels of service that had been achieved by the publicly run company. There were also various implementation milestones (including investment) and reporting requirements, such as the submission of annual reports on the location of areas of flooding risk. Each of the standards had a monetary penalty that could be imposed by the municipality in the case of noncompliance by the concessionaire.

Tariff Setting

The concession agreement contained detailed provisions for the setting of tariffs. These base tariffs are adjusted annually to take account of price inflation, using an indexation mechanism involving the consumer price index, wage index, electricity price index, and Bulgarian lev-euro exchange rate. Tariffs may also be adjusted due to certain eligible events, such as specific types of change in law or additional costs incurred by the concessionaire due to differences between the actual quality of the raw water supplied to the concession company and the contractual assumptions.

Dispute Resolution

In order to resolve disputes that might arise between the Municipality of Sofia and Sofia Water, the contract sets out a nonbinding mediation procedure and a concession dispute resolution board with three jointly appointed members: a chairperson (a lawyer trained in arbitration), a technical expert, and a financial expert. There is also an appointing authority in the event the parties cannot agree on the selection of these members. If either party disagrees with a decision of the board, it can take the case to arbitration in Bulgaria within 30 days; otherwise, the decision automatically becomes binding. Arbitration is conducted under rules of the United Nations Commission on International Trade Law.

Contract Monitoring

When the concession agreement was drafted, there was no national water regulator in Bulgaria. However, the municipality recognized the importance of establishing a dedicated unit to monitor the concession's performance and control tariffs. Therefore, the concession agreement provided that an independent concession monitoring unit (CMU)—Omonit—would be established to monitor the concessionaire. The concession contract granted the CMU certain rights, responsibilities, and obligations vested in it by the municipality. In order for the CMU to be an effective regulatory tool, the establishment of the CMU was made a condition precedent to contract effectiveness. Thus both the concessionaire and the municipality had to agree on the scope and functions of the CMU according to the principles stipulated in the concession contract prior to the effective date.

Omonit was set up in 2001 as an independent organization acting on behalf of the municipality and the consumers. Omonit was created to be the primary point of contact for the concessionaire and to act as a technical body and adviser to the municipality, collecting information and carrying out an expert analysis of the concessionaire's performance. Omonit was created as an interim measure until such time as the regulatory framework was developed. The intent was that the regulatory function would effectively be "migrated" out of the concession contract itself, once a formal regulator was in place. However, Omonit was not created at the time of contract signature, so responsibility for making decisions under the concession agreement—for example, imposing penalties—remained with the municipality.[5]

Omonit was created as an independent entity to give it operational and financial autonomy from the administration and to allow it to recruit high-caliber experts at market-based salaries through five-year renewable contracts with the municipality. Through a competitive process, three Omonit directors were recruited: a technical expert, a customer service expert, and a financial expert, and by 2005 the company had 15 staff members. Omonit's annual budgets are funded through a surcharge on tariffs collected by the concessionaire on a pass-through basis.

The role of Omonit was crucial to ensure compliance of Sofia Water with the most important service standards, including water and wastewater quality. However, ambiguities and definitional gaps in the contract still led to disagreements between Omonit and Sofia Water. These disagreements ranged from how Sofia Water interpreted particular service standards to whether the company used correct methods to calibrate the network model.

---

[5] http://rru.worldbank.org/Documents/PapersLinks/Sofia&BorneoCaseStudy.pdf.

By 2005 a new law was passed to expand the jurisdiction of the Bulgarian energy regulator to the water sector. The State Energy Regulatory Commission became the State Energy and Water Regulatory Commission (SEWRC). SEWRC is now responsible for setting tariffs and monitoring the quality of services of enterprises in the gas, electric, district heating, and water supply and sewerage sectors. After the creation of a national regulator, Omonit became part of the Municipality of Sophia's structure, with clearly defined rights and duties. Omonit's role moved from the monitoring of service levels to a very tight monitoring of the condition of the assets. Sofia Water has the obligation, set out under the conditions of the concession agreement, to present to the municipality, twice a year, a general report and an updated asset register.

In 2008 the municipality and Sofia Water renegotiated part of the concession agreement to give Sofia Water more flexibility in the negotiation of tariffs. According to the latest agreements, the concessionaire now has the right to ask for an increase in the price of water under certain conditions. If those conditions are met but the SEWRC does not allow higher prices, the private company can cancel the concession agreement. Should this happen, the municipality will not be obliged to pay damages to Sofia Water, but it will have to cover all of its outstanding loans.

Key lessons of the project include the following:

- In the absence of a national water regulator, an independent well-resourced monitoring unit is needed to monitor the concession's performance and control tariffs (later replaced by a national regulator).
- The contract agreement needs to contain detailed provisions dealing with service standards and tariff adjustments together with performance targets such as, in this case, water leakage, drinking water quality, and pressure and effluent standards. Still, issues can arise with regard to the interpretation of certain obligations.
- The concession agreement also needs to set out a clearly defined dispute resolution procedure. This may involve the establishment of a dispute resolution board designed to resolve disputes that might arise between the public and private parties quickly and cost-effectively.
- Even so, the contract provisions and monitoring may not be enough to enable smooth running of the contract, especially in projects that involve user charges in politically sensitive sectors such as water, in which case a regulator, acting within a national framework, may be better placed to play this supervisory role.

11.

CONCLUSION

Public-private partnerships (PPPs) are an important tool for governments seeking to expand and improve the provision of infrastructure and other social services for their citizens. As such, they can help to boost economic growth and development and to fight poverty. PPPs have been used in developed countries in a wide range of sectors, and they are increasingly being seen as part of the menu of solutions to the lack of infrastructure service provision in developing countries. However, PPPs can fulfill this role only if they appropriately combine the interests of the two partners—that is, the interests of the government in expanding and improving services for citizens that are sustainable and achieving value for money and the interests of private investors in obtaining a reasonable return on their investment for the risks they are being asked to bear. Engaging in successful PPPs requires policy makers who have foresight and vision in deciding how the PPP program fits with their broader development agenda. Preparing and managing PPP projects take time, resources, and specific skills. Bringing sound PPP projects to the market and establishing an enabling environment that will contribute to their long-term sustainability are particularly important. Investors are highly selective, and financial resources have become increasingly scarce in this post-crisis world. Citizens have also become more vocal in demanding rapid, concrete results and tangible evidence of improvements in the delivery and quality of public services.

This guide provides a road map of the tasks for governments in developing countries interested in tapping the potential of the private sector to advance their development agenda through the use of PPPs. It highlights the dimensions—legal, financial, commercial, technical—that need to be tackled at different points of the PPP process, from laying the framework, to a project's inception, and eventually to ensuring that the required service is actually delivered over the duration of the contract. The guide introduces the reader to the substantive discussions on the options available to policy makers seeking to address each dimension of the PPP process and the issues that are likely to be raised at each stage, providing case study examples of how these obstacles have been overcome. It highlights the benefits of taking a program, rather than a project by project, approach wherever possible. It shows that a PPP is not just a financial transaction: with its focus on better risk allocation over the long term, it can be a more efficient procurement tool available to governments for the delivery of a public service. PPPs usually involve a radical shift in approach to the way public services are procured and delivered. However, the impact of this change can often be underestimated by governments and the private sector. The guide aims to provide a realistic view of what is involved so that these changes are better understood and managed earlier on.

In addition to the "what," the guide provides an understanding of the "how" of PPPs in infrastructure. Specific institutional arrangements need to be made to translate political will into an actual program of PPP projects that will be well received by investors and the public at-large. The book examines the various options open for making those arrangements, such as appointing interagency commissions or creating separate public sector PPP units. It also describes how other broader tools and institutions, such as PPP laws or regulatory entities, are needed to ensure the long-run success of PPPs: the importance of understanding their impact on the transaction at hand at an early stage of project preparation, their role in ensuring the coherence and consistency of the PPP program, and their role in providing clarity in the rules over the lifetime of the project.

That said, implementing successful PPPs ultimately relies on the abilities of the individuals tasked with making them work. The availability of specific skills needed to prepare, launch, and manage PPPs can represent a major implementation challenge in developing countries. How to address this issue will depend on the degree of economic and institutional development of the country, and the solutions will vary accordingly. Governance of the process is key. In building this road map, this guide also highlights at each stage the types of skills that are needed, the kinds of advisers required, and how they should be managed to complement and strengthen the government team. Having the right mix of skills is vital to the credibility of the program. It also strengthens the negotiating position of the government vis-à-vis the private sector and facilitates consultations and communication with the public at-large on the benefits of developing a strong PPP program and in ensuring that the right projects get implemented.

Partnerships between the public and private sector can make a significant contribution to improving the living standards of citizens and enhancing the competitiveness of the economy. The case study presented in chapter 5 illustrates some of these achievements using the Manila Water Company as an example and how, over 13 years, the company achieved substantial improvements in services and an increase in coverage to 98 percent of the concession area. In chapter 1, the example shows how combining private participation and increased competition in Colombian ports in the 1990s led to dramatic improvements in service performance.

To reap the benefits of PPPs involves a careful and complex preparation process—and often patience—as final results may take time to materialize after the contract has been signed. The actual terms of those contractual agreements and the changes needed to create an enabling environment will depend on the country, the sector, and often the specific transaction. At the same time, the steps needed to get there are always the same: they constitute a frame of reference, a necessary point of departure for countries to succeed with their PPPs. The present guide aims to present this framework as a whole and to highlight the requirements, the options, and the challenges that governments are likely to face in developing the framework so that a successful PPP program can be implemented and the benefits for both partners—public and private—can be fully realized.

WORLD BANK AND PPIAF PRIVATE PARTICIPATION IN INFRASTRUCTURE PROJECT DATABASE

The World Bank and PPIAF Private Participation in Infrastructure (PPI) Project database is divided into sectors as follows:

- Energy (electricity and natural gas)
- Telecommunications
- Transport (airports, seaports, railways, and toll roads)
- Water and sewerage (treatment plants and utilities).

It does not include social infrastructure projects and therefore excludes most private finance initiative (PFI models) PPPs (see chapter 2). Within these four sectors, the database identifies four types of projects: management and lease contracts, concessions, greenfield projects, and divestitures.

Management and Lease Contracts

In management and lease contracts, a private entity takes over the management of a state-owned enterprise for a fixed period, while ownership and investment decisions remain with the state. There are two subclasses of management and lease contracts:

- *Management contract.* The government pays a private operator to manage the facility, while the operational risk remains with the government.

- *Lease contract.* The government leases the assets to a private operator for a fee, while the private operator takes on the operational risk.

These contracts share some, but not all, of the characteristics of public-private partnerships (PPPs) as defined in this guide.

Concessions

In concessions, a private entity takes over the management of a state-owned enterprise for a given period, during which it assumes significant investment risk. The database classifies concessions according to the following categories:

- *Rehabilitate, operate, and transfer (ROT).* A private sponsor rehabilitates an existing facility and then operates and maintains the facility at its own risk for the contract period.
- *Rehabilitate, lease or rent, and transfer (RLT).* A private sponsor rehabilitates an existing facility at its own risk, leases or rents the facility from the government owner, and then operates and maintains the facility at its own risk for the contract period.
- *Build, rehabilitate, operate, and transfer (BROT).* A private developer builds an add-on to an existing facility or completes a partially built facility, rehabilitates existing assets, and then operates and maintains the facility at its own risk for the contract period.

All of these would be concession PPPs as defined in this guide.

Greenfield Projects

In greenfield projects, a private entity or a public-private joint venture builds and operates a new facility. If there is a contract, the facility may, or may not, be transferred to the public sector at the end of the contract period. The database identifies five types of greenfield projects:

- *Build, lease, and transfer (BLT).* A private sponsor builds a new facility largely at its own risk, transfers ownership to the government, leases the facility from the government, and operates the facility at its own risk up to the expiration of the lease. The government usually provides revenue guarantees through long-term take-or-pay contracts for bulk supply facilities or minimum-traffic revenue guarantees.
- *Build, operate, and transfer (BOT).* A private sponsor builds a new facility at its own risk, operates the facility at its own risk, and then transfers the facility to the government at the end of the contract period. The

private sponsor may or may not own the assets during the contract period. The government usually provides revenue guarantees through long-term take-or-pay contracts for bulk supply facilities or provides minimum-traffic revenue.

- *Build, own, and operate (BOO).* A private sponsor builds a new facility at its own risk and then owns and operates the facility at its own risk. The government usually provides revenue guarantees through long-term take-or-pay contracts for bulk supply facilities or minimum-traffic revenue guarantees.
- *Merchant.* A private sponsor builds a new facility in a liberalized market in which the government provides no revenue guarantees. The private developer assumes construction, operating, and market risk for the project (for example, a merchant power plant).
- *Rental.* Electricity utilities or governments rent mobile power plants from private sponsors for periods ranging from one to 15 years. A private sponsor places a new facility at its own risk and owns and operates the facility at its own risk during the contract period. The government usually provides revenue guarantees through short-term purchase agreements such as a power purchase agreement for bulk supply facilities.

The first two of these subcategories would be PPPs as defined in this guide. In addition, even though the third one, build, own, and operate (BOO), is not strictly speaking a PPP, the content of this guide is relevant, because the procedures to select, prepare, and bid this type of arrangement are similar to what is discussed in the guide.

Divestitures

In divestitures a private entity buys an equity stake in a state-owned enterprise through an asset sale, public offering, or mass privatization program. The database identifies two types of divestitures:

- *Full.* The government transfers 100 percent of the equity in the state-owned company to private entities (operator, institutional investors, and the like).
- *Partial.* The government transfers part of the equity in the state-owned company to private entities (operator, institutional investors, and the like). The private stake may or may not imply private management of the facility.

These would not be PPPs as defined in this guide.

SAMPLE EXTRACT OF A RISK MANAGEMENT REGISTER FOR MANAGING THE PPP PROJECT PROCESS

XYZ Project Risk Register: General
Updated on XYZ

Identification number	Owner	Date identified	Date last updated	Risk description	Risk status	Impact	Comments	Mitigating action	Target date	Actual closure date	Current risk status	Risk to
1	X	1/4/2007	7/9/2007	Late commissioning of advisers	Medium	High	Draft scope of service and tender as soon as possible in order to meet the end of February deadline	Scope of services to be drafted by end of January, tender documents to be issued by early February, tenders received by mid-February, appointment of consultants by end of February	5/2007	6/2007	Closed	Program management
2	X	1/4/2007	1/2/2008	Inadequate central team staff resource	Medium	High	Monitor requirements	Avert issues for in-house information and communications technology adviser and central support unit lawyer	4/2008	Ongoing	Unchanged	Program management
3	X	1/4/2007	7/9/2007	Technical support not up to speed	High	High	Clarify quality and capacity of consultants; determine a process for measuring consultant's performance	Appoint consultants	5/2007	5/2007	Closed	Program management
4	Legal team	1/4/2007	1/2/2008	Land issues for project sites	High	High	Identify issues associated with any of the sites that can have an adverse impact on costs and scheduling of works for the whole program, such as owner-ship of site, covenant, contamination, and utilities issues	Program surveys as soon as possible in order to ascertain positions and condition of sites	3/2008		Unchanged	Program management

Identification number	Owner	Date identified	Date last updated	Risk description	Risk status	Impact	Comments	Mitigating action	Target date	Actual closure date	Current risk status	Risk to
5	Project board	1/4/2007	12/3/2008	Affordability	High	High	Flag funding gaps, if any, as soon as possible and identify other sources to support the program; alternatively scale down size of the works	Identify other sources, scale down works, request larger funding envelope	11/2009		Unchanged	Final business case
6	X	1/4/2007	12/3/2008	Difficulties with stakeholder buy-in	Medium	High	Secure in principle agreement letters; more work required for samples	Hold training sessions with XYZ, clarify project scope, begin to develop communications strategy	3/2008		Reducing	Outline business case
7	X	1/4/2007 (revised, 12/15/07)	12/3/2008	Completion of comprehensive building and ground surveys	Medium	High	Conduct high-quality surveys for high-risk areas; address concerns regarding condition survey warranties	Conduct further surveys	Ongoing		Reducing	Procurement
8	X	1/4/2007	1/2/2008	Late submission of outline business case	High	High	Change central support unit guidance, for example, on planning and surveys		1/2008		High	Outline business case
9	X	1/4/2007 (revised, 12/15/07)	1/2/2008	Outline planning consent (sample schemes)	Medium	High	Await outcome of planning applications	Provide additional information as required	4/2008		Reducing	Outline business case
10		1/4/2007	7/9/2007	Changes to reorganization plans	Low	Medium	Undertake statutory reorganization process	Ensure good consultation	6/2008		Unchanged	Project outcomes

(continued next page)

Identification number	Owner	Date identified	Date last updated	Risk description	Risk status	Impact	Comments	Mitigating action	Target date	Actual closure date	Current risk status	Risk to
11	X	1/4/2007	7/9/2007	Weak communication strategy leading to reduced confidence in plans	Medium	Medium	Ensure regular communications	Assign responsibilities	4/2007	5/2007	Unchanged	Program management
12	X	1/4/2007	7/9/2007	Employee transfer issues	Medium	High	Clarify employee transfer issues	Discuss issues with XYZ	7/2008		Unchanged	Procurement
13	X	1/4/2007	7/9/2007	Internal resources not identified (for example, legal, finance)	Medium	Medium	Plan additional posts	Draw up recruitment plans	5/2007		Closed	Program management
14	X	1/4/2007	1/2/2008	Abnormal funding issues	Medium	High	Continue reviewing abnormal costs		1/2008		Closed	Outline business case
15	Finance team	1/4/2007	1/2/2008	Sign off of XYZ	Medium	High	Calculate funding and agreement scheme for each project component	Appraise options	2/2008		Closed	Outline business case
16	Finance team	1/4/2007	1/2/2008	Value added tax and other tax issues	Low	High	Assess impact on affordability if not resolved	Have finance team meet with in-house value added tax team to ensure that the scope of services does not affect the council's partial exemption	2/2008		Closed	Procurement

Identification number	Owner	Date identified	Date last updated	Risk description	Risk status	Impact	Comments	Mitigating action	Target date	Actual closure date	Current risk status	Risk to
17	Tech team	1/4/2007	1/2/2008	Inherent latent defects	Medium	High	Conduct more detailed condition surveys; consider contingency position	Commission further surveys where potential risks are identified	9/2008		Unchanged	Procurement
18	Tech team	1/4/2007	1/2/2008	Highway risks leading to increased costs and delays	Medium	Medium	Consider construction traffic, accessibility, further works	Hold technical discussions; traffic review for outline business case	9/2008		Unchanged	Procurement
19	X	1/4/2007	1/2/2008	Inadequate change in management plans	Medium	High	Undertake staff development to support changes	Develop project change plans further with advisers	3/2008		Reducing	Project outcomes
20	X	1/4/2007	10/3/2008	Lack of interest in projects from bidders	Medium	High	Address the small number of private finance initiatives	Hold open day for market testing and schedule XYZ conference; develop enhanced marketing strategy	6/2008		Increasing	Procurement
21	X	1/4/2007	1/2/2008	Design and development	Medium	Medium	Assess the quality of designs	Engage client's design adviser	Ongoing		Unchanged	Procurement
22	X	1/4/2007	12/3/2008	Phasing of work	Low	Medium	Decide how to handle increased procurement costs	Discuss with bidders; model options	03/2008		Complete	Outline business case
23	Finance team	7/9/2007	1/2/2008	Interest rate changes	Medium	Medium	Consider possible changes in projects due to fluctuating factors	Be prudent at outline business case; monitor closely, updating affordability	Ongoing		Unchanged	Procurement

(continued next page)

Identification number	Owner	Date identified	Date last updated	Risk description	Risk status	Impact	Comments	Mitigating action	Target date	Actual closure date	Current risk status	Risk to
24	X	7/9/2007	12/3/2008	XYZ statutory notices (if required)	Low	Medium	Land disposals and siting of new project components	Hold early dialogue with ministry	Ongoing		Reducing	Outline business case
25	X	7/9/2007	1/2/2008	Risk of challenge from unsuccessful bidder	Low	High	Follow procurement guidance	Develop robust procedures, audit trail of dialogue, and dialogue protocol	11/2009		Unchanged	Procurement
26	X	7/9/2007	1/2/2008	Need to vary standard documentation	Low	Medium	Stay with standard documentation where possible	Hold regular dialogue with public-private partnership center	Ongoing		Unchanged	Procurement
27	X	7/9/2007	1/2/2008	Perception risk	Medium	High	Obtain strong leadership and political commitment	Determine messages and approach to bidder's event; hold dialogue with bidders	Ongoing		Unchanged	Procurement

Source: Authors.

LIST OF PPP WEB SITES

Region or country	Organization	Web site
Africa and Middle East		
Regionwide	Infrastructure Consortium for Africa	http://www.icafrica.org/en/
Egypt, Arab Rep.	Ministry of Finance, PPP unit	http://www.pppcentralunit.mof.gov.eg
Mauritius	Ministry of Finance, PPP unit	http://www.gov.mu/portal/sites/ncb/ppp/index.htm
South Africa	National Treasury, PPP unit	http://www.ppp.gov.za/
The Americas		
Brazil	Ministry of Planning, PPP unit	http://www.planejamento.gov.br/hotsites/ppp/index.htm
	Estruturadora Brasileira de Projetos	http://www.ebpbrasil.com/ebp/web/default_eni.asp?idioma=1&conta=46
	Minas Gerais state government PPP portal	www.ppp.mg.gov.br
	São Paulo state government PPP portal	http://www.planejamento.sp.gov.br/PPPEngl/ppp.aspx

(continued next page)

Region or country	Organization	Web site
Canada	Partnerships British Columbia	http://www.partnershipsbc.ca
	Infrastructure Ontario	http://www.infrastructureontario.ca
	Canadian Council for Public-Private Partnerships	http://www.pppcouncil.ca
	PPP Canada	http://www.p3canada.ca/home.php
	Infrastructure Quebec	http://www.ppp.gouv.qc.ca/index.asp?page=home_en&lang=en
Chile	Ministry of Public Works	http://www.mop.cl/servicios/Paginas/Concesiones.aspx
Colombia	Ministry of Finance	www.minhacienda.gov.co
	National Planning Department	www.dnp.gov.co
Mexico	Ministry of Finance PPP portal	http://www.pps.sse.gob.mx/html/desarrollo.html
	Programa para el Impulso de Asociaciones Público-Privadas en Estados Mexicanos	www.piappem.org
Peru	Proinversión	www.proinversion.gob.pe
Puerto Rico	PPP Partnerships Authority	http://www.p3.gov.pr/?lang=en
United States	Federal Highway Administration, Public-Private Partnerships	http://www.fhwa.dot.gov/PPP/
	National Council for Public-Private Partnerships	www.ncppp.org
Asia and Pacific		
Regionwide	Asian Development Bank, Private Sector Operations Department	http://www.adb.org/PrivateSector/Finance/default.asp

(continued next page)

Region or country	Organization	Web site
Australia	New South Wales Treasury, Working with Government	http://www.treasury.nsw.gov.au/wwg/
	Partnerships Victoria	http://www.partnerships.vic.gov.au
	South Australia	http://www.treasury.sa.gov.au/dtf/infrastructure_support/projects_branch.jsp
India	Ministry of Finance, PPP unit	http://www.pppinindia.com
	Planning Commission, Committee on Infrastructure	http://infrastructure.gov.in/
	National Highways Authority	www.nhai.org
Japan	PPP cabinet office	http://www8.cao.go.jp/pfi/e/home.html
Korea, Rep.	Private Infrastructure Investment Management Center	http://www.pimac.org/
	Korea Development Institute	http://www.kdi.re.kr/kdi_eng/main.jsp
Pakistan	Infrastructure Project Development Facility	www.ipdf.gov.pk
Singapore	Ministry of Finance, PPP unit	http://app.mof.gov.sg/ppp.aspx
Europe		
Regionwide	European Bank for Reconstruction and Development	Report on best international practices in public-private partnerships with regard to regional policy issues: http://www.ebrd.com/country/sector/law/concess/ppp/atkins.pdf

(continued next page)

Region or country	Organization	Web site
	European Commission	Guidelines for successful public-private partnerships: http://ec.europa.eu/regional_policy/sources/docgener/guides/ppp_en.pdf
		Resource book on PPP case studies: http://ec.europa.eu/regional_policy/sources/docgener/guides/pppresourcebook.pdf
	European Investment Bank	Role of the European Investment Bank in public-private partnerships: http://www.eib.org/projects/publications/the-eibs-role-in-public-private-partnerships-ppps.htm
		European PPP Expertise Centre (EPC): http://www.eib.org/epec/index.htm
Belgium	Vlaams Kenniscentrum Publiek-Private Samenwerking	Public-private partnership process approach: http://www2.vlaanderen.be/pps/english/process_eng.html
Czech Republic	PPP Centrum	Useful documents: http://www.pppcentrum.cz/index.php?cmd=page&id=1197
France	Ministère de l'Économie et des Finances, Mission d'Appui PPP/PPP task force	http://www.ppp.minefi.gouv.fr/
Germany	Partnerschaften Deutschland, PPP task force	http://www.partnerschaften-deutschland.de/en/
Greece	Ministry of Economy and Finance, special secretariat for PPPs	http://www.ppp.mnec.gr/en
Ireland	Department of Finance, central PPP policy unit	http://www.ppp.gov.ie
Italy	Unità tecnica Finanza di Progetto, PPP task force	http://www.utfp.it/default_eng.htm

(continued next page)

Region or country	Organization	Web site
Netherlands	PPP Knowledge Centre	http://kenniscentrumpps.econom-i.com/uk/pps/home_frameset.html
Poland	Centrum PPP	http://www.centrum-ppp.pl/start,2
Portugal	Parpública, PPP task force	http://www.parpublicasgps.com/
Russian Federation	Vnesheconombank PPP Center	http://www.veb.ru/en/PPP/
Scotland	Scottish government, financial partnerships unit	http://www.scotland.gov.uk/Topics/Government/Finance/18232
	Scottish Future's Trust	www.scottishfuturestrust.org.uk
United Kingdom	Her Majesty's Treasury	U.K. general PPP/PFI guidance: http://www.hm-treasury.gov.uk/ppp_index.htm
	Partnerships UK / Infrastructure UK	U.K. general PPP/PFI guidance: www.partnershipsuk.org.uk
	National Audit Office	Value-for-money reports: http://www.nao.org.uk/recommendation/reportList.asp
	Local Partnerships	Local government PPP guidance: http://www.localpartnerships.org.uk/
	Office of Government Commerce	Procurement guidance, gateway processes: www.ogc.gov.uk/what_is_ogc_gateway_review.asp
	Department of Health	http://www.dh.gov.uk/en/Aboutus/Procurementandproposals/Publicprivatepartnership/Privatefinanceinitiative/index.htm
	Community Health Partnerships	http://www.communityhealthpartnerships.co.uk/
	Partnerships for Schools	www.partnershipsforschools.org.uk/
	Highways Agency	www.highways.gov.uk/roads/2992.aspx

(continued next page)

Region or country	Organization	Web site
	Department for Environment, Food, and Rural Affairs	Waste infrastructure delivery program: http://www.defra.gov .uk/environment/waste/residual/ widp/index.htm

Other multilateral agencies

Nongovernmental organizations	Bank Information Center	International financial institution transparency resource: www .ifitransparencyresource.org/
Other	Global Public-Private Partnerships in Infrastructure portal	http://info.worldbank.org/etools/ PPPI-Portal/
	International Finance Corporation	http://www.ifc.org/
	Multilateral Investment Guarantee Agency	http://www.miga.org
	PPP in Infrastructure Resource Center	http://www.worldbank.org/ pppiresource
	Private Infrastructure Development Group	http://www.pidg.org/
	Public-Private Infrastructure Advisory Facility	http://www.ppiaf.org/
	World Bank Institute	http://web.worldbank.org/WBSITE/ EXTERNAL/WBI/WBIPROGRAMS/PPPI LP/0,,menuPK:461142~pagePK:641 56143~piPK:64154155~theSit ePK:461102,00.html
United Nations agencies	United Nations Commission on International Trade Law, Procurement, and Infrastructure Development	http://www.uncitral.org/uncitral/en/ uncitral_texts/procurement _infrastructure.html

(continued next page)

Region or country	Organization	Web site
	United Nations Economic Commission for Europe	http://www.unece.org
Consultants	E.R. Yescombe, PPP consultant	Comprehensive list of international PPP Web sites and a bibliography of links to PPP-related publications and research: www.yescombe.com

Source: Authors.

REFERENCES

Africa Partnership Forum. 2007. "Investment: Unlocking Africa's Potential." Briefing Paper 2, Africa Partnership Forum, Paris.

Bakovic, Tonci, Bernard Tenenbaum, and Fiona Woolf. 2003. "Regulation by Contract: A New Way to Privatize Electricity Distribution?" Energy and Mining Sector Board Discussion Paper 7, World Bank, Washington, DC.

Brown, Ashley, Jon Stern, and Bernard Tenenbaum, with Defne Gencer. 2006. *Handbook for Evaluating Infrastructure Regulatory Systems*. Washington, DC: World Bank.

Delmon, Jeffrey. 2009. *Private Sector Investment in Infrastructure: Project Finance, PPP Projects, and Risk*. Washington, DC: Kluwer and PPIAF.

———. Forthcoming 2011. *Public-Private Partnership Projects in Infrastructure: An Essential Guide for Policymakers*. New York: Cambridge University Press.

Eberhard, Anton. 2007. "Matching Regulatory Design to Country Circumstances: The Potential of Hybrid and Transitional Models." Gridlines Note 23, PPIAF, Washington, DC. May.

———. 2008. "Tailoring Regulatory Institutions to Local Needs and Resources." World Bank workshop, Washington, DC. November 5.

Gaviria, Juan. 1998. "Port Privatization and Competition in Colombia." Public Policy for the Private Sector Note 167, World Bank, Washington, DC. December.

4Ps. 2002. "Soft Market Testing Exercises and How to Undertake Them." In *4Ps Know-How*. London: 4Ps.

Gratwick, Katharine Nawaal, and Anton Eberhard. 2006. "An Analysis of Independent Power Projects in Africa: Understanding Development and Investment Outcomes." University of Cape Town, Graduate School of Business, Cape Town.

Guasch, J. Luis. 2004. *Granting and Renegotiating Infrastructure Concessions: Doing It Right*. Development Studies. Washington, DC: World Bank Institute.

Harris, Clive, and Kumar Patrap. 2008. "What Drives Private Sector Exit from Infrastructure?" Gridlines Note 46, PPIAF, Washington, DC.

Hodges, John T., and Georgina Dellacha. 2007. "Unsolicited Infrastructure Proposals." Gridlines Note 19, PPIAF, Washington, DC. March.

ICA (Infrastructure Consortium for Africa) Secretariat. 2006. *Infrastructure Project Preparation Facilities: User Guide—Africa*. Tunis: ICA Secretariat.

India, Ministry of Finance. 2007. "Model Request for Qualification for PPP Projects." In *Guidelines of the Ministry of Finance, Government of India*. New Delhi: Ministry of Finance.

Ipsos Mori Social Research Institute. 2009. *Investigating the Performance of Operational Contracts*. London: Ipsos Mori. March.

Irwin, Timothy. 2007. *Government Guarantees: Allocating and Valuing Risk in Privately Financed Infrastructure Projects*. Washington, DC: World Bank.

Leigland, James, and William Butterfield. 2006. "Reform, Private Capital Needed to Develop Infrastructure in Africa: Problems and Prospects for Private Participation." Gridlines Note 8, PPIAF, Washington, DC.

Leigland, James, and Chris Shugart. 2006. "Is the Public Sector Comparator Right for Developing Countries?" Gridlines Note 4, PPIAF, Washington, DC. April.

Mandri-Perrott, Cledan. 2009. *Public and Private Participation in the Water and Wastewater Sector: Developing Sustainable Legal Mechanisms*. Water Law and Policy Series. London: IWA Publishing.

Matsukawa, Tomoko, and Odo Habeck. 2007. "Review of Risk Mitigation Instruments for Infrastructure Financing and Recent Trends and Developments." PPIAF Trends and Policy Options 4, PPIAF, Washington, DC.

Maurer, Arizu, Luiz Maurer, and Bernard Tenenbaum. 2004. "Pass Through of Power Purchase Costs: Regulatory Challenges and International Practices." Energy and Mining Sector Board Discussion Paper 10, World Bank, Washington, DC.

Pardina, Martin Rodriguez, Richard Schlirf Rapti, and Eric Groom. 2007. "Accounting for Infrastructure Regulation: An Introduction." World Bank, Washington DC.

Pardina, Martin Rodriguez, and Richard Schlirf Rapti. 2007. "Regulatory Requirements under Different Forms of Utility Service Delivery." World Bank and PPIAF, Washington, DC.

Partnerships Victoria. 2001. *Technical Note: Public Sector Comparator*. Melbourne: Partnerships Victoria.

———. 2003a. *Contract Management Guide*. Melbourne: Partnerships Victoria.

———. 2003b. *Supplementary Technical Note: Public Sector Comparator*. Melbourne: Partnerships Victoria.

Peterson, George. 2009. "Unlocking Land Values to Finance Urban Infrastructure." Trends and Policy Options 7, World Bank and PPIAF, Washington, DC.

Sanghi, Apurva, Alex Sundakov, and Denzel Hankinson. 2007. "Designing and Using Public-Private Partnership Units in Infrastructure: Lessons from Case Studies around the World." Gridlines Note 27, PPIAF, Washington, DC.

Schur, Michael, Stephan von Klaudy, Georgina Dellacha, Apurva Sanghi, and Nataliya Pushak. 2008. "The Role of Developing Country Firms in Infrastructure: New Data Confirm the Emergence of a New Class of Investors." Gridlines Note 3/35, PPIAF, Washington, DC.

Shugart, Chris, and Ian Alexander. 2009. "Tariff Setting Guidelines: A Reduced Discretion Approach for Regulators of Water and Sanitation Services." Working Paper 8, PPIAF, Washington, DC.

Sirtaine, Sophie, Maria Elena Pinglo, J. Luis Guasch, and Vivien Foster. 2005. "How Profitable Are Infrastructure Concessions in Latin America?" PPIAF, Washington, DC.

South Africa, National Treasury. 2004a. *PPP Manual: Module 3; PPP Inception.* Pretoria: National Treasury.

———. 2004b. *PPP Manual: Module 4; PPP Feasibility Study.* Pretoria: National Treasury.

———. 2004c. *PPP Manual: Module 6; Managing the PPP Agreement.* Pretoria: National Treasury.

United Kingdom, Her Majesty's Treasury. n.d. *Public Sector Business Cases Using the Five Case Model.* London: Her Majesty's Treasury.

———. 2004. *Value for Money Assessment Guidance.* London: Her Majesty's Treasury.

———. 2006. *Value for Money Assessment Guidance.* London: Her Majesty's Treasury.

———. 2007. *Operational Taskforce Note 2: Project Transition Guidance.* London: Her Majesty's Treasury.

United Kingdom, National Audit Office. 2006. *A Framework for Evaluating the Implementation of Private Finance Initiative Projects.* Vol. 1. London: National Audit Office.

———. 2009. *Private Finance Projects: A Paper for the Lords Economic Affairs Committee.* London: National Audit Office. October.

United Kingdom, Office of Government Commerce. 2005. "Market Sounding." In *Successful Delivery Toolkit.* London: Office of Government Commerce.

———. 2007. *OGC Gateway Process Reviews 0–5.* London: Office of Government Commerce.

von Klaudy, Stephan, Apurva Sanghi, and Georgina Dellacha. 2008. "Emerging Market Investors and Operators: A New Breed of Infrastructure Investors." Working Paper 7, PPIAF, Washington, DC.

Woolf, Fiona. 2009. "The Role of Regulation in Regional Markets and Infrastructure." Unpublished mss. PPIAF, Washington, DC.

World Bank and PPIAF (Public-Private Infrastructure Advisory Facility). 2001. *Toolkit: A Guide for Hiring and Managing Advisors for Private Participation in Infrastructure.* Washington, DC: World Bank and PPIAF.

———. 2002. "Emerging Lessons in Private Provision of Infrastructure Services in Rural Areas: Water and Electricity Services in Gabon." World Bank and PPIAF, Washington, DC. September.

———. 2009. "Assessment of the Impact of the Crisis on New PPI Projects." PPI Data Update Note 24, PPIAF, Washington, DC. October.

———. 2010. "Assessment of the Impact of the Crisis on New PPI Projects: Update 6." PPI Data Update Note 36, PPIAF, Washington, DC. May.

Yescombe, E.R. 2002. *Principles of Project Finance*. San Diego: Academic Press.

———. 2007. *Public-Private Partnerships: Principles of Policy and Finance*. Oxford: Butterworth-Heinemann.

INDEX

Boxes, figures, notes, and tables are indicated by *b*, *f*, *n*, and *t*, respectively.

energy, investment shares in, 3
environmental risks, 46
Equator Principles, 87, 87n
equity investment, 57
European Bank for Reconstruction and
    Development (EBRD), 139–40
European Investment Bank, 26
European Union, "competitive
    dialogue" in, 120–21
Europe Arab Bank, 101
export credit agencies, 62–63
expression of interest (EoI)
    documents, 119

F
"final business case," 77
financial assessment, 87
financial crisis of 2008–09, 1, 2f, 61
financing, 6, 53–76
    bankability
        contract terms, 6, 57
        lenders and risk, 54–57, 56b
    case studies
        São Paulo Metro Line 4, Brazil,
            47–48, 61, 69–73
        water services in East Zone
            of Metro Manila, Philippines,
            68, 69–75, 147
    contractual relationships, 57–59,
        58b, 59f
    debt underpinning, 63
    equity investment, 57
    export credit agencies, 62–63
    foreign currency risk, 48
    funding, other sources of, 65–66
    guarantees
        full-credit or "wrap"
            guarantees, 62
        other forms of, 65
        partial-credit guarantees, 62
        political risk guarantees and
            guarantee funds, 63–65
    output-based aid (OBA), 67–69
    overview, 53–54
    for project preparation, 84–85
    public sector–funded development
        banks, 66
    refinancing, 59–61

risk mitigation, 61–67
viability gap funding, 37, 66–67
"first in, last out principle," 53, 60
foreign currency risk, 48
framework, 6, 15–30
    implementation, 23–26
    investment, 21–23
    legal and regulatory, 16–21, 22f
    policy rationale, 15–16
    summary of recommendations, 26–27
    water and electricity in Gabon
        (case study), 16, 28–30
full-credit or "wrap" guarantees, 62
funding. *See* financing

G
Gabon, electricity and water
    (case study), 16, 28–30
"gateway" process in public sector, 83
gearing or leverage, 53
Global Partnership on Output-based
    Aid (GPOBA), 68, 74, 75
governance of projects, 80–82, 81f, 82b
greenfield projects, 3, 150–51
guarantees
    full-credit or "wrap," 62
    guarantee funds, 63–65
    other forms of, 65
    partial-credit, 62
    political risk, 63–65

H
Hankinson, Denzel, 23–24
highways, national sector, India
    (case study), 22, 82, 89–91
Hospital Regional de Alta
    Especialidad del Bajío,
    Guanajuato State, Mexico
    (case study), 38, 50–52
hospitals
    Hospital Regional de Alta
        Especialidad del Bajío,
        Guanajuato State, Mexico (case
        study), 38, 50–52
    Inkosi Albert Luthuli Central
        Hospital, South Africa
        (case study), 112–13,
        120, 124, 126–31

www.ingramcontent.com/pod-product-compliance
Lightning Source LLC
Chambersburg PA
CBHW070400200326
41518CB00011B/2002